Teacher Expectations in Education

The influence of teacher expectations on student outcomes is routinely explored by professors, administrators, teachers, researchers, journalists, and scholars. Written by a leading expert on teacher expectations, this book situates the topic within the broader context of educational psychology research and theory and brings it to a wider audience. With chapters on the history of the teacher expectation field, student perceptions of teacher expectations, and implications for practice, this concise volume is designed for use in educational psychology courses and any education course that includes social-psychological aspects of classrooms in the curriculum. It will be indispensable for student researchers and both pre- and in-service teachers alike.

Christine M. Rubie-Davies is Professor of Education and is in the Faculty of Education and Social Work at the University of Auckland, New Zealand.

Ed Psych Insights
Series Editor: Patricia A. Alexander

Assessment of Student Achievement
Gavin T. L. Brown

Self-Efficacy and Future Goals in Education
Barbara A. Greene

Self-Regulation in Education
Jeffrey A. Greene

Strategic Processing in Education
Daniel L. Dinsmore

Cognition in Education
Matthew T. McCrudden and Danielle S. McNamara

Emotions at School
Reinhard Pekrun, Krista R. Muis, Anne C. Frenzel, and Thomas Goetz

Teacher Expectations in Education
Christine M. Rubie-Davies

CHRISTINE M. RUBIE-DAVIES

Teacher Expectations in Education

NEW YORK AND LONDON

First published 2018
by Routledge
711 Third Avenue, New York, NY 10017

and by Routledge
2 Park Square, Milton Park, Abingdon, Oxon, OX14 4RN

Routledge is an imprint of the Taylor & Francis Group, an informa business

© 2018 Taylor & Francis

The right of Christine M. Rubie-Davies to be identified as author of this work has been asserted by her in accordance with sections 77 and 78 of the Copyright, Designs and Patents Act 1988.

All rights reserved. No part of this book may be reprinted or reproduced or utilised in any form or by any electronic, mechanical, or other means, now known or hereafter invented, including photocopying and recording, or in any information storage or retrieval system, without permission in writing from the publishers.

Trademark notice: Product or corporate names may be trademarks or registered trademarks, and are used only for identification and explanation without intent to infringe.

Library of Congress Cataloging-in-Publication Data
A catalog record for this book has been requested

ISBN: 978-1-138-69786-7 (hbk)
ISBN: 978-1-138-69787-4 (pbk)
ISBN: 978-1-315-52048-3 (ebk)

Typeset in Joanna MT
by Apex CoVantage, LLC

To Nesrin, a wonderful high expectation teacher, and Altan, an inspirational coach and mentor.

Contents

Acknowledgements		viii
One:	**The Beginnings and Development of the Teacher Expectation Paradigm**	**1**
Two:	**Teacher Expectations, Teacher Interactions, and Student Perceptions**	**31**
Three:	**Student Characteristics as Precursors to Differential Teacher Expectations**	**61**
Four:	**Teacher Differences in Propensity for Expectation Effects**	**109**
Five:	**What Has Been Learned and Where To Next?**	**143**
Glossary		152
Index		156

Acknowledgements

I would like to acknowledge those who, in many, many ways, have contributed to this book coming to fruition.

I would first like to thank Professor Patricia Alexander, who believed in me enough to invite me to write this book as part of her inspirational series. Teaching is in my heart; books like this enable me to write in ways that are accessible to teachers. I hope that in this writing just one teacher who reads this book will become a high expectation teacher. Ever the teacher, the chance to contribute positively to students is my major academic goal.

Special thanks must go to the reviewers of my first draft who provided excellent feedback and helped to substantially improve the book. To that end, I would also like to thank my daughter, Nesrin, an amazing teacher who took time out of her busy schedule to read through the final draft for me. Her help, at a critical time, was very much appreciated.

I am also indebted to Dan Schwartz, the editor on this project, for his patience and helpful guidance along the way.

I am extremely grateful to the many extraordinary high expectation teachers that I meet when I am out in schools. It is people like you who have ability and the belief in students to make classrooms equitable – places where talent is nurtured and not lost. It is you who provide the opportunities for every student in your care to succeed at the highest levels – particularly those normally regarded as disadvantaged. You show what students can achieve when teachers believe in them and implement high expectation principles.

Finally, to my family, and especially Jeff, my husband. Thank you for keeping me sane, for ensuring that I do things other than work, for believing in me, and for contributing so much to my joy in life.

One

The Beginnings and Development of the Teacher Expectation Paradigm

Many years ago teaching was thought to be easy, particularly at the elementary school level. Further, it was commonly believed, decades ago, that individual teachers did not make much difference to student learning because student achievement largely depended on families and their characteristics. Intelligence was thought to be hereditary and, therefore, it was thought that teachers did not have much influence on their students' learning.

Over time, research showed that teaching was extremely complex. It is the only profession where all "clients" are seen all together, at the same time, and every day of the working week; teachers are constantly multi-tasking and making immediate decisions. Researchers also came to recognize that some teachers had considerably more impact on student progress than did others. Research showed that teachers could make a difference to students' learning and that some were more effective than others. One contributing factor that can promote student learning is teacher expectations. Teacher expectations are the beliefs that teachers hold about the level of achievement students are likely to achieve in the future. Over time, it was found that the expectations that teachers hold can have consequences for what they teach, how they teach, how they interact with students, and how students become aware of these expectations and differential practices. The beliefs and practices that emanated from teacher expectations led to students learning more or less, depending on their teachers' expectations for them. This book will present the understandings that have been gained over the past five decades related to teacher expectations.

Studies of teacher expectations normally do not focus directly on the instructional and effective teaching methods that may be associated with achievement. Instead they are embedded within investigations of the social influences in classrooms and schools that impact student achievement. What is studied tends to be teacher beliefs about student ability to learn and the interpersonal processes between teachers and students that shape schooling outcomes. Teacher expectations and the research that has flowed from the study of this phenomenon is, therefore, a study of relationships and their significance for student learning. This book tells the story of this hugely important research paradigm in education and the processes that are involved. It leads us to the conclusion that teacher expectations are of vital significance in shaping student learning.

Much of the teacher expectation research has focused on teacher effects on individual students, with teacher data aggregated across classrooms. So, the findings are most often based on means for teacher behaviors across all the classrooms in any study. It is important from the outset, however, to recognize that, almost from the inception of the field,[1] it has been acknowledged that teachers vary enormously. That is, some teachers have far greater expectation effects on their students than do others. Teachers differ as much as students. Some teachers have far more positive expectation effects on students than others, some teachers are more swayed by stereotypical information than others, some teachers have high expectations for all their students, and so on. Hence, although the first three chapters mostly present research findings where the data from all teachers has been aggregated, clearly individual teachers differ, and, no doubt, some of the teachers from your own schooling stand out for one reason or another. Some of those reasons may have to do with teacher expectations. Think for a moment – who were your favorite teachers? Why? Do you remember perceiving expectations from your teacher that indicated whether they thought you were a strong or weak student? Did you have teachers who had similar expectations for all students or did they expect more from some students than from others? Do you remember any specific comments or actions directed towards you as a student? How did you feel?

In this first chapter, I discuss the rich history and beginnings of teacher expectations research that has included more than a thousand studies being conducted on the topic. I share how this research began and trace its complexity over history, including the positive ways in which teachers can communicate their expectations that then stimulate student achievement. The second chapter presents the research that has examined whether or not teachers differ in their interactions with, and behaviors towards, students for whom they have high or low expectations. This was the major direction of research immediately following the initial *Pygmalion* study (which will be introduced in the current chapter). The third chapter describes the research that has investigated a wide range of student characteristics that have been found to influence teacher expectations. Studies such as these ask questions like, what student information do teachers take account of in forming their expectations? The fourth chapter takes a different tack by exploring studies that have focused on teachers, rather than students, and has asked questions such as, are there some teachers who have greater or lesser teacher expectation effects on their students? Why is that? What are the particular characteristics of such teachers? The fifth chapter concludes the book. It draws together the findings presented throughout, discusses what we have learned from five decades of research into teacher expectations, how any negative effects of teacher expectations might be eliminated, and what further research needs to be undertaken.

4 The Teacher Expectation Paradigm

Expectation research began with the work of Merton.[2] In 1948, he proposed the idea that when people held an erroneous idea about other people or even institutions, as a consequence, they interacted with those people in ways that caused their initial beliefs to become true. Merton named this phenomenon the self-fulfilling prophecy effect. He gave a number of examples in his book that illustrated well how stereotyping and prejudice could be fueled and false beliefs could become reality. To use an educational example, in the earlier parts of the 20th century, it was believed that those of African descent were of lesser intelligence than white people. Remembering that schools were segregated in the US for many years, this led to the decision in at least one US state that less money would be allocated to educating black students, since they were not likely to benefit from education anyway. Because black students received an inferior education, they learned less than white students, thus perpetuating the belief that they were of lesser intelligence. However, although the concept of expectations and the self-fulfilling prophecy were introduced in the late 1940s, it was not until the 1960s that the idea was investigated in relation to education.

It is now almost 50 years since the first ever teacher expectation research, affectionately known as the *Pygmalion* study.[3] This study came into being in the middle of the Civil Rights Movement in the United States. Many students, particularly those from poor neighborhoods and those disadvantaged in other ways, were failing in school – or, perhaps it should be said, school was failing them. Moreover, although traditionally it had been believed that education could do little to alter what were thought to be innate traits, there became an increasing awareness that the environment could also have an effect on student achievement. Evidence was mounting that teachers could have marked effects on student learning and their influence could be positive or negative. These findings led to conclusions that the education system was not delivering an equitable education to all students. Some (mostly White middle class students) were being advantaged by the system whereas others (most notably, at the time, those from low socioeconomic areas, African American students, and other culturally and linguistically diverse students) were being disadvantaged.

Education has often been seen as a vehicle by which students who are prepared to work hard can change the life chances of themselves and their families. If the system does not facilitate this, then it is an unfair and unjust system. Teacher expectations were viewed as one means by which teachers may inadvertently advantage some students or create detrimental effects for others. For example, in one study,[4] the researchers showed that teachers had higher expectations for White students than they did for African American students, even though achievement was similar. After just one semester, the White students were given higher grades than the African American students, even though standardized testing showed that the achievement for both groups did not differ significantly. Over time, the teachers gave the White students more advanced work than the African American students such that, by the end of just one year, the White students were achieving at higher levels, thus fulfilling the teachers' original expectations.

As outlined earlier, realizing a person's expectations is described as a self-fulfilling prophecy. For example, within a particular classroom, a teacher may be getting a new student into her class, Paul. The teacher previously taught Maria, Paul's older sister. Maria did very well in the teacher's class so, before she has even met Paul, the teacher decides that Paul is likely to do just as well as Maria. This is despite information from Paul's former teacher that he is unsettled, difficult to motivate, and is achieving at average levels. The teacher decides that the former teacher has been giving Paul work that is too easy for him and that some of what he has been given has not interested him, and so that is why he is only achieving at average levels. When Paul begins school in his new class, the teacher interacts with him positively, encourages him in reading, mathematics, and other subjects, and provides him with effective teaching supports. She monitors Paul's learning closely so that he keeps making progress, and she includes learning experiences that tap into his interests. As a result, by the end of the year, Paul is achieving at similar levels to how Maria was when she was in the teacher's class. Hence, the teacher's originally false belief (that Paul was a high achiever like Maria) led her to interact with Paul in ways that affirmed to Paul that he was smart, such that by the end of the year, he was achieving at higher levels than he had done in the previous year.

It is important to acknowledge, at this point, that everybody forms expectations of others. Similar to stereotyping, forming expectations for how another person (or people) is likely to behave or interact is a means of reducing the complexity of the information that we are receiving when we meet others. Our expectations enable us to better guide our current and future actions and interactions. Problems arise when these expectations are false, negative, and are held rigidly, leading to the stultifying of another's potential. This applies as much in industry as it does in education. Although this book focuses on teacher expectation effects, there is clear evidence of expectation effects in realms outside the classroom.[5] And, it is important to remember throughout this book that there are some teachers who have much greater expectation effects than others.

THE EARLY WORK OF ROBERT ROSENTHAL

Robert Rosenthal had conducted a number of studies in the early 1960s where he had shown that experimenters could inadvertently influence the results of their laboratory experiments. For example, several of his experiments involved training rats to go through a maze. There were no differences in how smart the rats were. Rosenthal found that if the laboratory assistants were told that the rats they were working with were smart; the rats actually did learn to go through the maze more quickly than if laboratory assistants were told that the rats were not very smart. Rosenthal proposed that the rats must have been handled more gently and treated more kindly by the laboratory assistants when they thought the rats were smart, and more roughly and with less care when the laboratory assistants thought that the rats were not smart.

However, when he conducted the same experiments with rats in Skinner boxes, Rosenthal got the same results. The Skinner box had a maze embedded in it and rats learned to tap a lever once they reached the end of the maze in order to obtain food. When using Skinner boxes, the laboratory assistants did not actually touch the rats, and yet the results were the same. Nevertheless, Rosenthal proposed that there must have been something in the way that the laboratory assistants interacted with the rats while training them that led the rats to learn more quickly or more slowly, depending on whether the laboratory assistants had been led to believe that the rats were smart or not.

In a paper that Rosenthal published,[6] he proposed that if laboratory assistants could affect the learning of rats, perhaps the expectations of teachers could have an effect on their students. In other words, if teachers thought that particular students would do well in their class, perhaps they were nicer and more encouraging towards them than if the teachers thought that other students were likely to struggle and need a lot of support. It happened that Lenore Jacobson, a school principal, read the article that Rosenthal published and offered her school as the site for the first ever teacher expectation study.

8 The Teacher Expectation Paradigm

THE *PYGMALION* STUDY

In the Pygmalion study, all the children in Oak Elementary School were given an IQ test that was not well known. Rosenthal and Jacobson dressed it up in a fancy cover with a Harvard logo on it (which was where Rosenthal was based at the time) and called it *The Harvard Inflected Acquisition Test*. It was administered to every child in the school at the end of one school year. Teachers were not told that it was an IQ test; instead, they were told that it was a test that could predict students who would suddenly blossom and do really well at school. At the beginning of the following year, Rosenthal and Jacobson randomly selected 20 percent of students in the school to become the bloomers and gave the teachers the names of those students. In this way, the researchers planted a seed in the teachers' minds. They led the teachers to believe that some students in their class would do better than they had before; the researchers raised the expectations of the teachers for the randomly selected students.

All the students in the school were then tested at the end of the first year of the study. Across the whole school, those students who teachers had been told would suddenly bloom did perform at higher academic levels than the other students. This will be further discussed below. However, although Rosenthal and Jacobson appeared to have shown that expectations did exist in classrooms, the findings from the study brought both detractors and defenders. The detractors argued that it was not easy to influence student IQ, although the researchers had measured student achievement as well as IQ and found the same results. The detractors also criticized aspects of the way the study had been conducted. For example, Rosenthal and Jacobson suggested that teachers must have interacted differently with the bloomers causing them to improve, but they had not observed the teachers in their classrooms so they did not actually know if that was the case or not. Further, Rosenthal and Jacobson could not attest with any degree of certainty that teachers had actually taken the false expectations on board. As well, the detractors pointed out that although there was an overall effect across the school, actually the largest effects were with the youngest students in the school, those in Grades 1 and 2. Interestingly, the detractors did not question the existence of expectations; instead, they concentrated on critiquing the way the study had been conducted and some of the conclusions.

On the other hand, the defenders perhaps credited the study with more than was due. For example, some used the study as evidence to explain why disadvantaged students were not doing well in school – their lack of success was due entirely to their teachers' expectations of them. The defenders argued that teachers had low expectations for minority groups and those from low socioeconomic areas, and so that influenced student achievement. However, this is a negative connotation in relation to expectations (low expectations have a negative effect on student performance) and Rosenthal and Jacobson had not induced low expectations; they had manipulated positive expectations. Just because high expectations could increase student academic performance did not necessarily mean that low expectations would have a detrimental effect. However, the study made headlines in some newspapers and magazines, for example, *The New York Times, The New Yorker* and the *Reader's Digest*. The findings led one school system in the US to banish tracking, and the study was cited in court cases around educational issues such as the use of IQ tests to categorize students.[7] Nevertheless, whether detractor or defender, all seemed to accept the possibility that teacher expectations existed and, in some classrooms in particular, probably did have an effect on student outcomes.

THE TEACHER EXPECTATION PROCESS

The *Pygmalion* study led to a flurry of teacher expectation research, not least the classroom observational work by Brophy and Good,[1,8,9] which will be presented in more detail in Chapter Two. Their work led to a testable model for the communication of expectation effects in the classroom. Based on their earlier model, I have recently presented a more differentiated and expansive model[10] (which follows next) to demonstrate the teacher expectation process.

Teacher expectations work like this:

1) The teacher holds certain beliefs about the way in which education can best be delivered to the students in her care. For example, some teachers believe that their main role is to focus on the academic development of students whereas others believe that socialization and developing relationships among students is of key importance.
2) The teacher forms expectations for her students based on information she has been given about the students' previous achievement. This information may include both official records, specifying previous performance in different curriculum areas, as well as that passed on informally by other teachers. For example, a previous teachers' exasperation about a particular student, expressed in the staff lounge, could affect another teacher's expectations of that student when she finds that same student in her class the next year.
3) In accordance with the teacher's beliefs about how students should best be taught, coupled with her expectations, the teacher plans opportunities for her students' learning. These learning opportunities can extend student learning considerably or can constrain learning, depending on the types of learning experiences that the teacher plans for the students. For example, the teacher may believe that all students can

The Teacher Expectation Paradigm 11

improve markedly and therefore plan challenging activities for all students. Another teacher may believe that those achieving at lower levels need far more support and so plan revision and skill-based activities for them but more independent activities for high achievers.

4) The teacher delivers the learning experiences that have been planned for the students. The instruction can be at an individual, group, or class level. The learning experiences may be challenging for students or students may find them easy. Students may work in ability-based or mixed ability groupings, or the teacher may prefer that students work independently.

5) Students learn what they have been given the opportunity to learn. That is, they complete the activities that the teacher has designed for their learning. These activities convey messages to students about their teacher's expectations for them, particularly in situations where some students are completing high-level activities and others are not. Students assimilate the teacher's expectations and, over time, come to achieve at the level at which the teacher expects them to. This is often because their learning experiences, the opportunities the students have for learning, reflect their teachers' expectations. That is, the learning experiences offered to students can lead them to make fairly rapid or much slower progress simply because of the types of activities they have been presented with and the learning opportunities the activities enable.

6) The students' achievement informs teachers about how well the students are progressing and what should be planned next for learning. For example, students completing challenging activities may be excited about their learning and work hard to complete the activities because they are stimulating and rewarding. The teacher perceives such students as motivated and engaged, and plans further high-level tasks for them. On the other hand, students who have been assigned low-level

tasks may find these boring or repetitious of what they have done before. Because they are bored and view the tasks as easy, they may not be motivated to complete them, may not engage fully in the tasks, and therefore may not finish them. The teacher may perceive that the students have been unable to complete the tasks and so will plan further similar low-level tasks.

Figure 1.1 shows the teacher expectation process. It should be noted that the dotted line from the student outcomes to the formation of expectations in the model is designed to show that the effect from the teacher to the student is greater than the effect from the student to the teacher. Because teachers plan students' learning opportunities and the delivery of the learning experiences, to a large extent they control what students learn, particularly when students are younger. And, once students are set on a particular learning trajectory, it is often difficult to interrupt the learning journey that they are on.

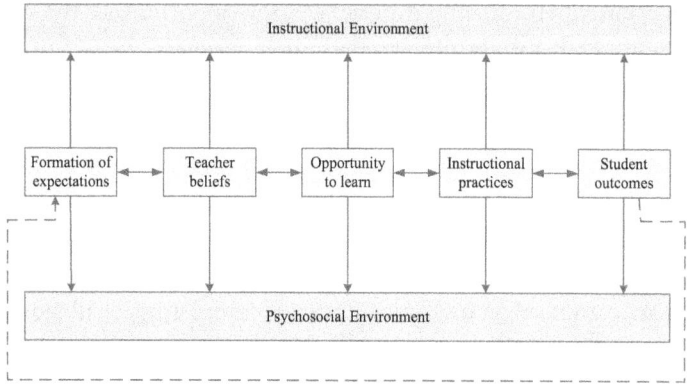

Figure 1.1 A model showing the teacher expectation process

This model originally appeared in Rubie-Davies, C. M. (2015). *Becoming a high expectation teacher: Raising the bar.* Reprinted with permission from Routledge.

The Teacher Expectation Paradigm   13

7) Student learning takes place both within the instructional environment and the psychosocial environment of the classroom. The instructional environment relates to the way in which the learning environment is structured. Do students sit in ability or mixed groupings, or do they sit in a more formal arrangement such as in rows or in a horseshoe? Do they work independently or cooperatively? Are all the learning experiences determined by the teacher or do students have a choice? How are new concepts introduced? What types of feedback does the teacher give to students? What types of tasks does the teacher provide to support student learning?

The psychosocial environment is really the class climate, that nebulous feeling in the air that is evident when an outsider walks into the classroom. Is the environment warm and emotionally supportive? What types of relationships does the teacher have with the students? Does she know each child personally? How does the teacher manage student behavior? How does she respond to students when they answer questions, particularly when the response is incorrect? How does the teacher motivate students? How does she emotionally support students' learning? How does the teacher ensure that students are engaged in their learning? How well do students relate to each other? Are students encouraged to support each other's learning or not? Is the teacher culturally responsive? How well accepted do all students feel?

Each one of these questions results in decisions by the teacher that will determine how both the instructional and psychosocial environments of the classroom are experienced by students. As with the opportunities for learning and the learning experiences available for students in the classrooms, both the instructional and the psychosocial environments of the classroom will convey messages to students about what their teacher expects of them. Some of these messages will be explicit, for example, telling some students that they are smart or are achieving well or received excellent marks on a test. On the other hand, others may be admonished for not doing well. I have been in classrooms where teachers have lists of the class reading levels on their classroom wall, with students' names next to their level. In such classes, each student's current achievement is very obvious to them and to everyone else. I wonder how it feels, as a student, to be one of those listed at the lowest level? I do not imagine such constant reminders are particularly motivating. Other messages will be more implicit, but will nevertheless be understood by students. For example, teachers may interact more warmly with those students for whom they have high expectations than with others; that is, they may be more emotionally supportive of such students. Although these differential interactions may be quite subtle, nevertheless, students notice. Through both the explicit and implicit messages of teachers, students learn their "place" in the class. They may also come to believe that some students are more valued than others. Later in this book, I will be describing in more detail the kinds of teacher behaviors that have been found to convey messages to students about whether or not their teacher has high or low expectations for them.

ACCURACY AND STABILITY OF TEACHER EXPECTATIONS

The effects of teacher expectations on student learning found in the *Pygmalion* study were modest and in many of the subsequent studies that took place in regular classrooms, the effects were also described as small or moderate. The most recent synthesis[11] of the results of almost 700 teacher expectation studies suggests that expectations have a medium effect on student achievement.

Some[12,13] have argued that teacher expectations are accurate and that they do not affect student learning very much; therefore, they are not worth considering. The idea here is that teachers can accurately judge where their students are up to and that they plan lessons accordingly. Interestingly though, the researcher[12,13] who most advocates that teacher expectations are accurate appears to do so on the basis that expectations do not affect student learning. The argument that teacher expectations are accurate is based purely on the idea that they do not affect student learning very much, therefore they must be accurate. Of course, the counter argument is that there is overwhelming evidence that, particularly in some circumstances, expectations can affect student outcomes to a noticeable degree. Of note, though, as will be explained later in this book, although expectation effects may be moderate when all classes are considered together, in some classes, in particular circumstances, and with some students, expectation effects can be quite large.

Among researchers[14] who have actually measured accuracy and then examined effects, their findings do not generally support the argument that teachers judge or estimate student achievement accurately. For example, in a Dutch study with over 11,000 students, where the degree of teacher accuracy was measured, teachers' expectations were found to be accurate for only about 33 percent of students. A similar result was found in a New Zealand study[15] with two separate samples of around 1500 students, where, again, accuracy was actually measured and, again, in both samples, teachers' expectations were found to be accurate for only about one-third of students. In another New Zealand study[16] of over 17,000 students, teacher expectations were found to be unacceptably inaccurate for particular groups of students (ethnic minority students, those from low socioeconomic groups, boys, and those with special needs) all of whom were given much lower ratings by their teachers than they deserved.

Hence, if expectations are inaccurate for many students, then to some extent, it might be assumed that teachers are planning for student learning from an erroneous base. Clearly, this does have consequences for students and their outcomes. For example, in the Dutch study mentioned above, students were tracked from primary school into secondary school based on their teachers' expectations of the track that they should be placed in. Because expectations were inaccurate for many of the students (when standardized achievement was taken into account), large numbers ended up in the wrong track. Ultimately, such errors in teacher expectations and judgement could affect students' life chances, because the track into which students are placed often predicts their ability to move into more prestigious and more highly paid occupations in adulthood. Within the Dutch system, the tracks into which students are placed determines their future types of occupations. Only the top track can move on to university, another track level leads to technical institutions and skilled occupations but the lowest tracks do not. Therefore, teacher track recommendations can be critical for students and their futures.

One of the earlier debates about whether teacher expectations existed and had effects on student learning, centered on studies that tried to replicate the findings of Rosenthal and Jacobson. Some of these were successful whereas others were not. Replication attempts were those where teachers were given false information about some students (that they were particularly smart students or that they would suddenly do well) and researchers then measured the outcomes. In some studies, student academic outcomes did increase but in others they did not. One researcher[17] decided to investigate more closely why the replications had been successful in some cases but not in others. He found that the time of the year that teachers were given the false information about students was important. If the suggestion that some students were very clever or that they would suddenly do very well was given to teachers within the first week of school, or before they even knew the students, then the experimental manipulation of teacher expectations worked and student outcomes were affected. However, if teachers were given the misleading reports more than two weeks into the schooling year, there were no effects on subsequent student outcomes.

It seemed that teachers formed their expectations within the first two weeks of school and, after that, even when they were given contradictory evidence by a researcher, they did not change their expectations. This suggested that teacher expectations may be fairly stable, once they have been formed. It was also suggested,[18] however, that even if teacher expectations were initially inaccurate, once teachers came to know their students, they would adjust their expectations in accordance with actual student achievement, and that therefore expectations were not likely to have large effects on student learning. The little evidence that there is about the stability of expectations does not seem to support this supposition but there have been only two studies[19,20] that have examined whether teachers' expectations do change over time. More evidence is needed in order to be able to say with any degree of certainty that expectations, once formed, are actually fairly stable. At the moment, it does seem that teachers tend to cling to their initial expectations even when they may be confronted with contradictory evidence. In the two studies that I did locate, the researchers reported that teacher expectations were stable. In one of those studies,[20] teachers rated each of their students on how well they expected them to perform on four different expectation variables: Overall performance, relationships with peers, cooperative class behavior, and ability to reason. Teachers were then asked to perform the same exercise eight weeks later. The researcher then explored the relations between teachers' earlier and later expectations. He found high levels of agreement between the first and second testing. Nevertheless, eight weeks is a relatively short time frame, and it could be argued that perhaps teacher expectations would not change much in that period. In the second study,[19] though, the authors collected teachers' expectations at the beginning of the year and then again, with two separate groups of students, six and eight months later. Overall, most teacher expectations were relatively stable across the school year. However, one interesting finding from this study was that expectations were more stable in some classes than in others. That is, there were some classes in which teachers did change their expectations for some students during the academic year, but there were others where there was little, if any change. Nonetheless, given that there have only been two studies that have explored the stability of teachers' expectations, no conclusions can really be drawn. This is an area where more research is needed. Researchers could explore not just whether expectations are stable but also whether they are more rigidly held for some students than for others. For example, it could be that teachers change or hold tight to their expectations for particular groups of students. It may also be that expectations are more rigidly held by some teachers than others. Both of these premises have yet to be investigated. The study just described seems to suggest that some teachers may be more flexible in terms of altering their expectations than others. It would be worth exploring what types of teachers adapt their expectations more than others, and why. It may be possible, in the future, to ascertain the types of teachers who are more rigid, and to provide professional development to help teachers become more objective in their assessments of students.

Currently, from what is known in the teacher expectation field, it seems that expectations are often inaccurate, and that once formed, they tend to be stable. Alarmingly, both these factors (inaccuracy and stability) appear to exist even when contradictory evidence is available and, as will be shown later in this book, it is often disadvantaged students who are the subject of teachers' inaccurate expectations, and for whom teachers seem to hold more rigid expectations. It is important that teachers use objective data to form their expectations and that they adjust their expectations as students progress and improve. There is no doubt that all teachers should have expectations; they need to because expectations are the basis on which teachers plan learning experiences for students, but they do need to be accurate.

LONG-TERM EFFECTS OF TEACHER EXPECTATIONS

As has been suggested, expectations can make a difference to student learning and these differences appear to be small to moderate. Hence, the effects certainly make a meaningful difference for students and, as has already been suggested, for some students and in some circumstances, the effects can be much larger. Moreover, one of the enduring concerns among researchers has been what the long term effects of teacher expectations might be. If teacher expectations make a difference of even 10 percent each year,[18] over time, as the effects compound, they could become much larger. Unfortunately, few studies in the teacher expectation field have tracked the effects of teachers' expectations on student achievement outcomes over more than one year so we know very little about whether or not the teacher expectation effects of one teacher, added to those of another, and so on, make larger differences in relation to student achievement than the effects that may occur within a single year.

One of the earlier studies in the teacher expectation field[21] illustrates how teacher expectation effects could compound over time. Ray Rist conducted a three-year observational study beginning when a group of 30 students began Kindergarten. The study was conducted in a poor urban setting and all students and teachers were African American. Prior to meeting her students, the Kindergarten teacher had information related to their prior attendance at a pre-school, a list of students whose families received welfare support, medical information, any parental concerns (obtained when parents registered the child for school), and the teachers' and her colleagues' previous experiences with any siblings. Hence, the information available to the Kindergarten teacher provided a social, rather than an academic profile, of each student.

By the eighth day of school, the teacher had placed the students into permanent seating arrangements. However, Rist observed that even earlier than that the teacher had begun favoring one particular group of students; they were chosen as leaders for a range of activities, were asked to read aloud, took part in "show and tell" more than other students, and were given responsibilities both within and outside the classroom. Hence, very early in their schooling career, one group of students, Table 1, appeared to be preferred over the others who were placed at Tables 2 and 3.

Rist noted that the students seated at Tables 2 and 3 appeared to differ from those at Table 1 in a number of ways. First, the physical appearance of those at Tables 2 and 3 was poorer and more unkempt than those at Table 1. Second, the students at Table 1 began to lead others in the class very early on and spoke confidently for the other students; they appeared relaxed with the teacher. Third, the Table 1 students interacted more frequently and more confidently with the teacher, whereas those at Tables 2 and 3 were more reticent and used non-standard American English more frequently than those from Table 1. Fourth, the teacher appeared to have also considered social factors when stratifying the students into groupings; overall, those seated at Table 1 came from homes where parent incomes were higher, where parent education was greater, and where family size was lower.

Rist argued that the teacher had developed expectations for the various students based on the four criteria above and then grouped them accordingly. Importantly, there had been no formal academic testing of the students when the teacher made her decision to group them at their tables. Once the teacher had

The Teacher Expectation Paradigm

assigned students to groups, she then differentiated the types of academic tasks they were given for the remainder of the year, as well as the ways in which she interacted with them. She interacted far more frequently with Table 1 and described them as her "fast learners" and, as the year wore on, mostly only ever called on Table 1 students to answer questions. Those at Tables 2 and 3 interacted with the teacher less and less, were more often excluded from class activities, and their instruction became more infrequent.

The detailed description above of the different lives of the students assigned to Table 1 versus those assigned to Tables 2 and 3 provided a platform for the students' future schooling. When 18 of the Kindergarten students moved to Grade 1 in the same school, all those from Table 1 the previous year were placed at Table A in Grade 1. Other than one child who was seated at Table C, all those from Tables 2 and 3 in Kindergarten were placed in Table B in Grade 1. Table C was made up of students repeating Grade 1, four new students, and the one student mentioned above. Because those from Table 1 in Kindergarten had been given more opportunities to learn during that year and had completed all the Kindergarten materials, at the beginning of Grade 1, they were immediately able to begin grade-appropriate work. On the other hand, those now at Table B had to spend the first weeks of school completing Kindergarten-level requirements before they were able to begin lessons at Grade 1 level. Similar to the Kindergarten teacher, the Grade 1 teacher appeared to have higher expectations for the Table A students than for the Table B or C students.

At the second grade level, three students from the original group had to repeat Grade 1, eight left and ten moved into Grade 2, where they were again assigned to three groups. Those from Table A all became Tigers in Grade 2 whereas those from Table B became Cardinals. The final, and lowest group, the

Clowns, was again comprised of students repeating Grade 2 and students new to the school. By this stage in the students' schooling, decisions about seating arrangements were based on reading achievement at the end of Grade 1. However, those in the Tigers group read more advanced books than those in the Cardinals who, in turn, were reading at a higher level than the Clowns. Further, school policy meant that all students needed to read a complete book before progressing to the next one, and the teacher did not allow any students to read ahead individually, such that they might complete a book earlier and advance; all students in each group had to read at the same pace. Therefore, it was impossible for any student from either the Cardinals or the Clowns group to be moved into a more advanced group no matter how well the student did. Rist described this as another form of self-fulfilling prophecy in that those ascribed to be slow learners were destined to remain so regardless of their potential or how well they performed during lessons. He concluded that the students' academic journey had been pre-ordained since the eighth day of Kindergarten.

As mentioned at the beginning of this section, we know very little about the effects of teacher expectations over time because there have been very few studies that have tracked the compounded effects of teacher expectations over a number of years, and no further studies since that conducted by Rist in 1970 that have collected such comprehensive observational data over several years. However, it must be remembered that Rist's data was qualitative and was collected from only three classrooms within one school. Although Rist's study seemed to provide evidence that teachers' expectations probably resulted in a self-fulfilling prophecy, he did not actually collect data on student achievement to show that the treatment of the lower level students had had a deleterious, and possibly permanent effect on their academic careers. Further, because the study was in one school, there were

The Teacher Expectation Paradigm 23

questions about whether or not the study was generalizable to other contexts. Moreover, the study has never been replicated. Finally, other studies in the expectation field suggest that teachers do not leave students in one permanent group but, instead, change students from group to group as they progress.[9,22] So while the descriptions that Rist provided are not in question, any conclusions in relation to his study must be cautious and tentative at most.

Some researchers[23,24] have collected teachers' expectations early in students' academic careers that have been either well above or well below students' actual academic performance. When achievement data has been collected several years later, students' academic performance has reflected that of the teacher expectations collected early in students' academic careers. These studies are investigating what can be termed carry-over effects. In other words, when a teacher has low or high expectations for a student compared to their achievement in one particular year, and the teacher's expectations affect the student's achievement, do those earlier inaccurate expectations still predict student achievement several years later? For example, in one study,[23] the researchers collected teacher expectations and student IQ when the students were only four years of age. They found that teachers tended to overestimate the ability of those with higher socioeconomic status and those perceived as being more confident and autonomous. That is, the teachers expected some students to do better than their grades at the time suggested that they would. On the other hand, teachers underestimated students from low socioeconomic backgrounds and those that they considered lacked maturity; they believed that the students would do worse than their current achievement indicated. Fourteen years later, the researchers found that the teacher over- or underestimation when the children were only four predicted their GPA and SAT scores when they were graduating from high school. It may be that classroom processes were at play which exacerbated the early inaccurate expectations of the teachers but this is unknown because no observations of the students were made. All that can be surmised is that when the teachers' expectations were inaccurate (either high or low) early in a student's schooling, even many years later the students were still fulfilling the expectations of the original teachers.

It is possible to imagine that the classroom lives of students at elementary school may differ depending on their teachers' expectations for them. I hinted at these differences earlier whereby students who are overestimated are placed in higher ability groups and given opportunities not available to those in the lower ability groups. On the other hand, those in the lower ability groups are not considered capable, and so are given lower level tasks to complete. But it is likely not just that opportunities to learn are differentiated that leads to the ever-widening gap between those considered high versus low achievers. Students know what groups they are in, no matter how teachers try to disguise them. Students can also come to see that there is a hierarchy such that those considered more able may also be considered more valued by the teacher. It must be incredibly frustrating to be confronted day after day with work that is easy and boring while you see your peers engaging in exciting, fun activities. It is perhaps little wonder that those students labelled as low achievers are often those who end up misbehaving in class, become de-motivated, and eventually drop out of school early. What a waste of talent!

At high school, it may be even more difficult to make up ground once you have been assigned to a lower track. At times a completely different curriculum is offered to students in high versus low tracks and so it becomes impossible to learn what you are not taught. One example of this, is the Dutch study[14] mentioned earlier. In the Netherlands, at the high school level, there are five tracks. Only the highest track prepares students for a college education. There is some opportunity for students to move tracks, but with a differentiated curriculum it becomes difficult. The basis on which students are assigned to tracks is the elementary school teacher's recommendation. Up until very recently, Dutch students did not have to sit a standardized test at the end of their primary schooling and, even if they did, teachers did not have to take account of the results because it was considered that factors other than achievement results (such as student effort) might determine student success at high school. Five years later, the track that elementary school teachers had recommended students be placed in predicted student achievement outcomes. Taking the original achievement, IQ and social factors like academic motivation into account, towards the end of high school, the difference in achievement between those who had been underestimated and those who had been overestimated was the equivalent of a whole school year's learning. For those students who were severely underestimated versus grossly overestimated, a negative bias seemed to be more damaging than a positive bias was helpful for student achievement. In this study, those from a low socioeconomic group and boys were more likely to be underestimated than were girls and middle class students. It would seem that a decision made at the end of elementary school may have affected the future life chances of, particularly, boys and those from low socioeconomic groups.

However, in the two studies described above, these are not compounded effects. That is, the researchers are not measuring the teacher expectations effects that occur in one year, added to the effects from the next year, and so on. Instead, they investigated carryover effects – whether the effect of, for example, students being misplaced in tracks, was reflected in their later achievement. There has only been one study[25] that has focused on the compounding of teacher effects. That is, the researchers investigated the idea that when the Kindergarten teacher over- or under-estimated student achievement, and then subsequent teachers also over- or under-estimated achievement of the same students that this would result in an overall compounding of teacher expectation effects. That is what was found. The more that students were overestimated by their Kindergarten and Grade 1 teachers, the greater were their achievement gains by Grade 4. Similarly, the more that students' achievement had been underestimated by subsequent teachers, the lower was their achievement by Grade 4. However, again in this study, no information on classroom processes or teacher interactions was collected and so it is unknown exactly what occurred in the classrooms that led to students increasingly achieving at higher or lower levels as the effect of teachers' expectations compounded from one year to the next. There are many possibilities. Teachers may have differentiated the work that students completed, leading to different student outcomes. Teachers may have favored some students more than others. Some students may have become disheartened.

Nevertheless, both the observational evidence as well as that showing teachers expecting some students to do better or worse than their actual achievement does suggest that early in students' academic career, the Kindergarten teacher seems to set students' achievement on a particular trajectory based on her expectations. The Grade 1 teacher then bumps that trajectory in a similar direction affecting achievement at Grade 1; the same pattern occurs at Grade 2, and so on. Over time, therefore, the differences in achievement between those for whom teachers have high versus low expectations can become exacerbated. It is possible that a teacher with very different expectations from those of any previous teacher could interrupt the upward or downward trajectory of students, but, to date, no such studies have been conducted, so we simply do not know whether the deleterious effects of one teacher's low expectations can be interrupted by the favorable

The Teacher Expectation Paradigm 27

expectations of another teacher. Within the teacher expectation field, the area of the long-term effects of teacher expectations is one where research could make an important contribution to understandings of the effects and processes of teacher expectations. This would be particularly so were both observational, expectation, and achievement data to be collected in the one study.

When I teach students at university and talk about expectations and their effects on student outcomes, I normally get students to think about (and possibly discuss) one teacher in their schooling career who had a significant positive or negative effect on their life chances, because of the teacher's expectations. Sometimes these are what Weinstein calls "critical incidents"[26] – one thoughtful or thoughtless comment that can have a marked effect on students' lives. I am always amazed at how many students will reveal in great detail such incidents, often with a lot of underlying emotion. Some of these stories are inspiring; some are disheartening. I have heard stories from students of a teacher who got alongside them, supported them, made them believe in themselves, such that they ended up succeeding in ways they never thought possible. But I have heard the opposite as well. For example, I recently heard the story of a young woman who said she had always wanted to be a veterinarian. When she was in high school, her physics teacher told her that she was hopeless at physics and would never get the grades to become a veterinarian. On the basis of that one comment, her dream dissipated and she had become a teacher instead. Of course, teaching is the most wonderful vocation so she chose wisely, but it was not the path this young woman had originally wanted to follow. I also recently heard of a young woman from an ethnic minority group who desperately wanted to be an engineer. Her school, in a low socioeconomic area, refused to allow her to take the mathematics courses that she needed in order to enter university because they said the courses would be far too difficult for her and she would fail anyway. Fortunately for her, she had a white middle class advocate, who, frustrated at the school's response, took her to another high school in a middle class area. They offered her the courses she needed. She is now in her third year of engineering at the top university in the country. Stories like these touch my heart. I am sure they resonate with all teachers who are passionate about their students and want to make a difference in their lives. Expectations and the processes and responses that follow can make a meaningful difference to students.

REFERENCES

1. Brophy JE, Good TL. Teachers' communication of differential expectations for children's classroom performance: Some behavioral data. *Journal of Educational Psychology.* 1970;61:365–374.
2. Merton RK. The self-fulfilling prophecy. *The Antioch Review.* 1948;8:193–210.
3. Rosenthal R, Jacobson L. *Pygmalion in the classroom: Teacher expectation and pupils' intellectual development.* New York: Holt, Rinehart & Winston; 1968.
4. Alexander KL, Entwisle DR. Achievement in the first 2 years of school: Patterns and processes. *Monographs of the Society for Research in Child Development;* Serial No. 218. 1988;53(2):1–157.
5. Eden D, Shani AB. Pygmalion goes to boot camp: Expectancy, leadership, and trainee performance. *Journal of Applied Psychology.* 1982;67:194–199.
6. Rosenthal R. On the social psychology of the psychological experiment: The experimenter's hypothesis as unintended determinant of experimental results. *American Scientist.* 1963;51:268–283.
7. Spitz HH. Beleaguered Pygmalion: A history of the controversy over claims that teacher expectancy raises intelligence. *Intelligence.* 1999;27: 199–234.
8. Brophy JE, Good TL. Teacher-child dyadic interaction system. *Mirrors for behaviour: An anthology of observation instruments continued.* Vol A. Philadelphia: Research for Better Schools, Inc; 1970.
9. Brophy JE, Good TL. *Teacher-student relationships: Causes and consequences.* New York: Holt, Rinehart & Winston; 1974.
10. Rubie-Davies CM. *Becoming a high expectation teacher: Raising the bar.* London: Routledge; 2015.

11. Hattie J. *Visible learning: A synthesis of over 800 meta-analyses relating to achievement.* London: Routledge; 2009.
12. Jussim L, Harber KD. Teacher expectations and self-fulfilling prophecies: Knowns and unknowns, resolved and unresolved controversies. *Personality and Social Psychology Review.* 2005;9:131–155.
13. Jussim L, Robustelli SL, Cain TR. Teacher expectations and self-fulfilling prophecies. In: Wentzel KR, Wigfield A, eds. *Handbook of motivation in school.* New York: Routledge; 2009:349–380.
14. de Boer H, Bosker RJ, Van der Werf M. Sustainability of teacher expectation bias effects on long-term student performance. *Journal of Educational Psychology.* 2010;102:168–179.
15. Rubie-Davies CM, Meissel K. A question of accuracy: Teacher expectations and the quest for equal educational opportunities (2017, May). Paper presented at the American Educational Research Association Annual Meeting, San Antonio: Texas.
16. Miessel K, Meyer F, Yao E, Rubie-Davies C. Subjectivity of teacher judgments: Exploring student characteristics that influence teacher judgments of student ability. *Teaching and Teacher Education.* 2017; 65: 48–60.
17. Raudenbush SW. Magnitude of teacher expectancy effects on pupil IQ as a function of the credibility of expectancy induction: A synthesis of findings from 18 experiments. *Journal of Educational Psychology.* 1984;76:85–97.
18. Brophy JE. Research on the self-fulfilling prophecy and teacher expectations. *Journal of Educational Psychology.* 1983;75:631–661.
19. Kuklinski MR, Weinstein RS. Classroom and grade level differences in the stability of teacher expectations and perceived differential treatment. *Learning Environments Research.* 2000;3:1–34.
20. Martinek TJ. Stability of teachers' expectations for elementary school aged children. *Perceptual and Motor Skills.* 1980;51:1269–1270.
21. Rist RC. Student social class and teacher expectations: The self-fulfilling prophecy in ghetto education. *Harvard Educational Review.* 1970;40:411–451.
22. Weinstein RS. Reading group membership in first grade: Teacher behaviours and pupil experience over time. *Journal of Educational Psychology.* 1976;68:103–116.
23. Alvidrez J, Weinstein RS. Early teacher perceptions and later student academic achievement. *Journal of Educational Psychology.* 1999;91:731–746.
24. Sorhagen NS. Early teacher expectations disproportionately affect poor children's high school performance. *Journal of Educational Psychology.* 2013;105:465–477.

25. Rubie-Davies CM, Weinstein RS, Huang FL, Gregory A, Cowan P, Cowan C. Successive teacher expectancy effects across the early school years. *Journal of Applied Developmental Psychology*. 2014;35:181–191.
26. Weinstein RS. *Reaching higher: The power of expectations in schooling*. Cambridge, MA: Harvard University Press; 2002.

Two
Teacher Expectations, Teacher Interactions, and Student Perceptions

As mentioned in the previous chapter, one question that arose from the *Pygmalion* study was whether or not teachers interacted differently with students for whom they held high or low expectations. At the time, it was thought that differential teacher interactions and behaviors towards high or low expectation students may have been one mechanism by which teachers directly or inadvertently let their students know what their expectations for them were. Researchers began to ask questions such as: Do teachers communicate their expectations to students? If so, how do teachers do this? Do some teachers communicate their expectations more so than others?

Following the work of Rosenthal and others, other researchers began to examine how teachers naturally formed their expectations for student achievement and how teacher expectations then impacted how they treated students that the teachers believed were more or less capable. Researchers were curious about teachers' own expectations rather than those that were artificially given to them. Jere Brophy and Tom Good[1-4] initiated a program to answer these questions by building a sophisticated observation system[1] that enabled them to record and measure the dyadic communication between teachers and individual students in ways that studied differences in quantity (e.g., frequency) and quality (e.g., difficulty of response opportunities) of interactions. Teachers were asked to rank their students in order of their perceived achievement (the teachers' expectations for each student). Then the researchers studied whether teachers treated students differently when they were believed to have more or less potential.

Strikingly, the careful observations of Brophy and Good showed that teachers did differentiate in the ways in which they interacted with their students. For example, a strong association was found between more favorable interaction patterns with students believed to be more capable. They were given more opportunities to respond to teacher questions than students for whom teachers had low expectations. Teachers also demanded much higher quality work from high expectation students than from lows, and gave them more feedback on their learning than they did low expectation students. Further, teachers praised high expectation students more than they did lows when they gave correct responses to questions, even though low expectation students provided the correct answer less often. Low expectation students were more likely to be criticized by teachers than were highs. Teachers were also more vigilant with regards to the behavior of low expectation students, particularly boys. Their behavior was much more closely monitored than that of girls or high expectation boys, and low expectation boys were frequently admonished by teachers for unsatisfactory behavior of one kind or another. Teachers were more likely to ignore the poor behavior of the other students even when they engaged in similarly disruptive behaviors.[3] Nevertheless, it should be noted that although Good and Brophy reported overall patterns in teacher-student interactions, the researchers noted individual differences in teachers as regard to the extent that they treated students differently.

However, after several years and many studies, a summary of the 17 main ways in which teachers overall (remembering that there were individual differences) discriminated in their behaviors towards high and low expectation students was documented.[5,6] These will be listed below and how these behaviors are portrayed in the classroom will be described.

PORTRAYAL OF HIGH AND LOW EXPECTATIONS THROUGH 17 TEACHER BEHAVIORS

The key teacher behaviors that differed towards high or low expectation students told students both directly and indirectly what their teachers' expectations for them were but, as will be shown, some of these behaviors could also be interpreted as providing more learning opportunities and support for high expectation students than for lows.

Wait time. Teachers waited less time for low expectation students to respond to questions than they did highs. This may have been because teachers expected highs to be able to produce a correct response, and so they waited more time for them when the students did not answer immediately. In relation to low expectation students, conversely, teachers may not have believed that the student could actually answer the question, even if the student had raised their hand. One reason that teachers may have waited less time could be because they did not want to embarrass the student by continuing to wait, when the teacher believed that the student would not be able to answer correctly anyway. However, a consequence was, that, over time, low expectation students were actually being given less time to think about an answer than were highs; arguably they may need more time to think and process a response. They should certainly be given the opportunity.

Question response. Given the finding above, it is perhaps not surprising that teachers also responded differently to high and low expectation students when they did not seem to know the answer to a question. When low expectation students were struggling with a response, teachers were more likely to either give them the answer themselves or to ask another child to answer instead. An alternative strategy could be to either repeat or rephrase the question, or to provide clues. These methods could help low expectation students to think more deeply and enable them to provide a correct response. From a social psychological perspective, as well, students are much more likely to feel positive and comfortable about responding when they know that they are likely to be supported to an answer, as opposed to either the teacher supplying the answer, or having another student respond. Both these latter responses provide subtle messages that the student is not capable of participating in the class at the required level.

Inappropriate reinforcement. One way in which teachers appeared to compensate for more frequent incorrect responses and lower level work from low expectation students seemed to be to reward them inappropriately. For example, instead of giving a low expectation student feedback that could result in the student being guided to a correct answer or facilitating their learning, the teacher might praise such students for their effort, even though the work produced was possibly low level, and lacked quality below what the student could achieve given appropriate support. Similarly, at times teachers commented on the behavior of low expectation students rather than on their learning and progress. They monitored the behavior of low expectation students very closely. Hence, the messages that teachers gave to low expectation students were confusing. On the one hand, they were being told that they had made a great effort or had behaved appropriately, but, on the other hand, they were not being given any opportunity to improve the standard of their work because no clear directions were provided.

Criticism. Teachers were also found to criticize low expectation students more frequently than highs when they made a mistake. Given that low expectation students were less successful than highs academically, this meant that they were criticized far

Expectations, Interactions, and Perceptions 35

more often than highs. At times such students were also belittled or humiliated by their teachers for making an error. Such teacher behavior gives students very clear messages about what their teacher thinks of them and is likely to lead to lower rates of responding for fear of the consequences.

Praise. Perhaps not surprisingly given the above finding, low expectation students were praised less frequently for success than their high expectation peers. Given that low expectation students were less often successful than highs, receiving even less praise than highs when they were correct seems downright mean! Again, this may serve to decrease the responses that low expectation students would be prepared to offer, when, if they are incorrect, they are likely to be criticized and, if they are correct, there are likely to be no rewards.

Feedback. Also in relation to teacher-student dyadic interactions, low expectation students were less likely to be given constructive feedback following responses to teacher questioning than were high expectation students. When high expectation students responded to teacher questions, teachers more frequently encouraged students to think more deeply or provided feedback that helped them to consolidate their learning. This happened far less frequently for low expectation students.

Attention. Overall, teachers were found to pay less attention to low expectation students generally. They interacted with them less frequently than they did high expectation students and they ignored them more often. It is possible that when students came to realize that their attempts to interact with the teacher were ignored, that they may have given up. They probably noticed that particular students were often called on and the teacher spent more time with those students than with them. This may have solidified views that some students in the class were more valued than others.

Choosing students. Teachers also called on low expectation students less frequently to answer questions than they did highs. It may be that teachers considered that the low expectation students would not be able to answer more difficult questions and so they simply did not ask them. It may be that the classroom was so busy that the teacher just wanted to get to a correct answer quickly and move on. Whatever the motivation, the end result was that some students were being given fewer learning chances than others and this was not acceptable in an education system that proclaimed equal educational opportunities.

Seating. Some studies[7] had found that the students for whom teachers had lower expectations were seated further away from the teacher than those for whom they had high expectations. Hopefully that does not happen in most classrooms nowadays! However, a related finding was that teachers tended to lean closer towards those for whom they had high expectations and remained more distant from those for whom their expectations were low. Body language is not so easily controlled so it may be that even if low expectation students are not now seated at a distance from teachers, that teachers still present body language that proclaims a distant relationship with the student.

Teacher demands. Overall, teachers demanded less from lows than they did from high expectation students. This could be evident in different ways. For example, teachers tended to teach more, to teach at a more rapid pace, and to provide briefer explanations with fewer repetitions and examples, when they believed that students would grasp the material. They were more likely to introduce new concepts more frequently. Ultimately, one group learned more than another largely because they had been given more opportunity to do so. Another way in which teacher demands were played out was that teachers were more likely to accept work of poor quality or incorrect responses from low expectation students than from highs. Lows were not pushed to produce work of higher quality when they may have been capable of doing better. There was perhaps also the student's perspective whereby they would see the poor quality work they had produced as acceptable to the teacher, in contrast to much higher quality work from other students that the teacher demanded be further improved. Again, over time, low expectation students are likely to understand these subtle messages.

Individualized interactions. Teachers tended to interact more frequently with high expectation students in public and with low expectation students in private. This may have been because the teachers believed that lows needed more support. However, it is likely to be the quality of the support that is important, rather than the quantity. Teachers also monitored low expectation students more closely and gave them more structured work than they did high expectation students. High expectation students were more likely than lows to be given more freedom in the types of activities that they completed, to be given higher level activities, and to be given more independence. Because high expectation students received more public attention, they may also have had more opportunities to receive the public acclaim of their teacher and peers. Low expectation students were also likely to become aware that they were being closely monitored by their teachers.

Grades and assignments. A further way in which teachers differentiated between high and low expectation students was in their grading of assignments and tests. Although decisions about the grades that students received should have been objective, where student work was borderline, teachers were more likely to assign higher marks or grades to those for whom they had high expectations and the opposite for lows. Practices such as these can serve to exaggerate the gap between high and low achievers, leading students to believe that they are doing better or worse than they actually are. As was shown in the previous chapter, many teachers are not particularly accurate in their assessment of students' levels of achievement.

Friendliness of interactions. Teachers not only criticized low expectation students more than they did highs, they were also less friendly in their interactions with lows. They smiled at them less frequently but frowned at them more often. Teachers were also shown to be less warm towards those for whom their expectations were low. If lows perceived these differences, then they may have believed that they were not as well liked as the high expectation students. Again, the nonverbal behavior of the teachers may have been portraying messages to students.

Student initiation. A further finding that complemented teacher-initiated questions was that when low expectation students asked their teachers a question, they were likely to receive a briefer and less informative response than were high expectation students. Considering that low expectation students were less likely to ask questions, if they received an unsatisfactory response from their teachers, this may have served to deter them even more from asking questions in the future. Again, this may have affected their learning. When they did have difficulties or wanted to understand or learn something, they may have become less and less likely to ask questions, depending on the teacher's reactions.

Eye contact. Not only have teachers been found to show less warmth towards low expectation students, they have also been shown to have less eye contact with them, and to display fewer behaviors indicating attention and responsiveness. For example, teachers did not lean towards low expectation students as much as they did towards highs, and they did not nod their heads as affirmation or agreement as frequently as they did when interacting with high expectation students. Again, teachers were providing subtle, nonverbal messages that they cared more for some students than they did for others.

Practice and revision. Similarly to some of the practices described above, low expectation students were much more likely to be given practice activities and revision via worksheets and what might be described as boring and mundane assignments. As a teacher once said to me with respect to catering for low achieving students, "They need to keep practicing their basic facts, day after day, until they get it." Such activities can hardly be described as inspiring and motivating, especially when contrasted with the types of learning experiences that high expectation students are being exposed to.

Effective instructional methods. One final way in which teachers were found to differentiate in the ways in which they treated high and low expectation students was that less effective instructional methods were often employed with low achievers. Effective teaching methods can take longer to implement and involve lengthier teacher-student interactions. When time is precious, teachers may have believed that they needed to push on with the curriculum even if this may have disadvantaged low expectation students.

I have deliberately written the above section in the past tense. Much of the work by Jere Brophy in relation to teacher expectations was carried out in the 1970s and early 1980s. It is hoped that at least some of the differential behaviors described above are no longer prevalent in today's classrooms. Indeed, it did seem, at the time, that teachers took note of the research findings and many made efforts to change their behaviors.[8] However, whether or not that awareness continues today is unknown. When you read through the listed and described behaviors, were there ones that made you stop and think about your own interactions? Were there behaviors that transmit expectations that you did not know about? Recently, I have been asked to give some presentations to teachers and school leaders specifically focused on these differential behaviors. This possibly suggests that teachers are not aware of how they may be sending subtle messages to students about their expectations for them. Latterly, it has been suggested[9] that there is very little, if anything, in teacher education textbooks, related to information about how teachers communicate expectation effects. Hence, currently we do not really know the degree to which teachers differentiate in their interactions with students for whom they have high or low expectations – remembering the caveat, that the behaviors listed above will be displayed to a greater or lesser degree by particular teachers. I hope that at least the behaviors and their explanations have made you think about your own practice.

Brophy and Good had mostly focused on the ways in which teachers' differentiated in their learning support of high and low expectation students. The differential learning support that low and high expectation students received served to explain why some students learnt more than others – in some classes, some students were being advantaged and some disadvantaged by the instructional practices of teachers. The focus in changing teacher practices fell on interacting more equally with students, and, as above, on distributing feedback more evenly and providing more learning support to low expectation students. Later, it was found,[10] however, that feedback, which was the easiest behavior for teachers to change, actually only had small effects on student outcomes. Instead, the emotional support that teachers provided coupled with the quality of the teaching were more important for student outcomes. Teachers not only discriminated in the ways in which students were supported in their learning, they also differentiated in their emotional support of students,[8,11] and this differential emotional support seemed to contribute more to student positive or negative outcomes than did the learning behaviors which had been the focus of research. Researchers were learning more and more about the teacher expectation paradigm.

TEACHER EMOTIONAL SUPPORT

There is some acceptance nowadays that teachers should give low expectation students more learning support than they do high expectation students. Lows begin further back and, therefore, they need some form of compensatory teaching if they are to have any possibility of achieving at the same level as high expectation students. This idea does not appear to be in dispute. Hence, teachers do make additional instructional efforts with low expectation students and may locate additional resources that they believe will further support student learning. Most teachers also endeavor to distribute their praise and feedback more equitably among students; some are more successful than others.

However, when the teaching of low expectation students is examined more closely, what is found is that teachers certainly spend more time teaching low expectation students and interacting with them, but the quality of the teaching is questionable; lows do not appear to receive the same quality of instruction as high expectation students.[11] Problems identified many years ago remain. For example, many teachers still do tend to provide lower level tasks to students for whom their expectations are low. They teach them at a slower pace, introduce new concepts gradually, and spend much time reinforcing concepts. Some teachers believe that low expectation students should not be asked questions requiring deep levels of thinking because they will not be able to answer the questions.[12] Of course, an unfortunate consequence of beliefs like this is that low expectation students are then not ever given the chance to develop their thinking. Such students often are not sufficiently challenged both in terms of the assignments they are given as well as in the interactions that they have with teachers; they could do better, given the opportunity. Instead, they may become bored and begin to cause behavioral disruptions. Differentiation in learning opportunities is further exacerbated in systems that advocate for within-class ability grouping or tracking.[13]

However, perhaps of more concern is differentiation in the emotional realm. Teachers are charged with the care of their students and while there may be some acceptance of differentiation within learning tasks, morally and ethically, the idea that teachers may favor some students more than others emotionally is difficult to justify. Yet this is what has been found across a large number of classrooms.[14,15] Some teachers tend to be warmer towards those for whom they have high expectations; it may be that they like them more.

From a human perspective, this is perhaps understandable. High expectation students are reinforcing of teachers' efforts because they achieve at high levels and they are usually engaged in learning. Highs also tend to be well-behaved and more easily managed by teachers. On the other hand, low expectation students may provide more challenges for teachers. Some are not well-behaved (perhaps they are bored), they tend to be less engaged in their learning, and teachers may struggle to help them learn concepts effectively.[11]

Whereas evenly dispensing feedback between high and low expectation students is relatively easy to monitor, controlling emotional expressions is much more difficult. The ability to control nonverbal displays varies between individuals and some nonverbal channels are easier to control than others. For example, whereas some people can control their facial expressions, with practice, controlling voice tone and body language is more difficult.[11] Thus, although teachers may not mean to, some may transmit more warmth to high rather than to low expectation students. Of course, trying to be overly sweet and nice towards low expectation teachers also does not work. Students are very adept at detecting genuine (and false) affective expressions.[8]

Over a number of years, Elisha Babad and his colleagues have conducted several studies[16–18] where they have investigated teacher nonverbal behavior and the ways that teachers portray their feelings to students. They used short 10-second video clips of teachers interacting with either a high or low expectation student. At times, the teacher was only talking about a particular student. Viewers could only see the teacher, not the student being spoken to or about. The viewers were asked to rate the teacher's nonverbal behavior. The researchers began by showing the clips to adults,[16] but later showed the same clips to students as young as nine years of age.[17,18] All groups (both adults and children) could tell from teachers' nonverbal behaviors whether the student the teacher was interacting with, or just talking about, was a high or a low expectation student. They knew from just a few seconds of video clip, whether or not the teacher liked the student they were talking to or not, and liking corresponded to whether the student the teacher was interacting with was high or low achieving. Perhaps even more interestingly, the final group of students[18] were from New Zealand and so they did not understand the Hebrew of the video-recorded teachers; they had to rely solely on the nonverbal behaviors of the teachers, yet they could still accurately determine whether the student being spoken to was a high or low expectation student.

Of course, as might be anticipated, some teachers discriminate more than others in their affection and emotional displays towards different students. This is not something that students accept; they do not like teachers who they perceive treat some students unfairly and inequitably. Whereas there is some acceptance by students of differential learning support, students do not hold the same perceptions when it comes to emotional support.[11] Students expect teachers to be fair and to treat all students similarly. When they do not this can affect the climate in the entire classroom.

In classes where teachers favor high expectation students over lows, the students are likely to feel less satisfied with their classroom, to report lower class morale, to react more negatively towards their teachers, to indicate that they do not wish to be with the same teacher the following year, and that they enjoy having a substitute teacher rather than their regular teacher.[15] In classrooms where teachers are perceived to have pets (the ultimate in teacher emotional differentiation), these student-reported feelings of dissatisfaction with their classes are likely to be even stronger. Teachers are in a position of power; students rely on them to treat everyone similarly, fairly and equitably.[11] It is important that teachers do not break the trust that is part of their profession and that they recognize the responsibility that they have for young people's lives.

As mentioned in the first chapter, the teacher expectation process occurs within the psychosocial environment of the classroom as well as the instructional environment. A positive psychosocial environment or class climate has frequently been linked to student satisfaction and higher achievement levels.[19–21] The class climate also contributes to student motivation and engagement. When students believe that teachers care about them personally and care about their learning, they are far more likely to put in greater effort and to want to please their teacher. In classrooms where the climate is warm, behavior problems tend to be reduced.

Making personal connections with students can help foster this sense of belongingness and teacher care. Just asking each child how their day is going or how their soccer game went, or how their mom is, can make a huge difference to student perceptions of how their teacher feels about them. Further, most classrooms in many Western countries are now ethnically diverse. It is important that every student feels accepted in the classroom, that they feel special, and that they belong. For example, in one school I recently visited, the teacher had 24 different nationalities in her class; the children spoke 18 different languages. The teacher could greet every child in their own language. That effort alone made the students feel special. Their faces glowed as she greeted each one and they responded. Further, the teacher also made the effort to connect with the children's families and their cultures. She regularly invited family members into the classroom to share some of their culture with all the students in her class. Some brought traditional food, some brought artefacts from their homeland, some spoke of the turmoil in their own countries that had led to them leaving, and some dressed up in national costume. This teacher also had a cultural day where all children brought their traditional food to share and dressed in a cultural outfit. The students plotted on a world map where they had come from and how they had arrived in their new country. In this class, every child felt loved and respected; they knew their teacher cared for them and they felt safe.

STUDENT PERCEPTIONS OF TEACHERS' EXPECTATIONS

Students are very aware of their teachers' expectations for them. They are extremely perceptive observers, and, at times, have been able to detail the ways that teachers interact differently with high and low expectation students that even trained observers have not detected.[11] Students notice what teachers say, they notice what teachers do, and they notice teacher nonverbal behaviors.[11,22] Rhona Weinstein has conducted a comprehensive research program whereby she has interviewed students about how they know about their teachers' expectations for them. She also developed an instrument to measure whether and how teachers systematically differentiated in the ways that they interacted with high and low expectation students.

Overall, the quantitative and qualitative findings together showed that many teachers seemed to differentiate in six key areas: Grouping for instruction, the types of activities students engaged in, the type of evaluation system used for assessment, how teachers endeavored to motivate students, the autonomy that students were given, and the quality of the relationships that the teacher encouraged in the classroom. The decisions that teachers make in terms of these six areas have consequences for the students. The teacher decisions can result in some students having very different educational experiences to those of others. They can also result in ability being made very salient in the classroom, or this information can be minimized. Further, opportunities to learn are enhanced or constrained depending on the teacher decisions in the six key areas outlined above. Each of these six areas and the consequences for students will be described below.

Grouping for instruction. Ability grouping appears to have a marked effect on student perceptions of whether or not they are smart. Despite teachers trying to disguise the level of particular ability groups by giving them creative names, students very quickly work out the hierarchy and know whether they are in a group considered to be smart or not. Students may even work out their actual place in class by determining where their group is in the hierarchy and then where they are within their group. Weinstein[22] describes a boy who says that he is 13th in his class through having used exactly that method. However, in classes that do not use ability grouping, the constant, daily messages about how smart some are compared to others become far more muted. Students may not be so aware of their relative smartness. Instead, all students are receiving messages about their individual progress and have perceptions that all students are doing well.

Classroom learning experiences. Another way in which students report that they know whether they are considered smart or not is through the kinds of tasks that they are assigned. Students know those who are assigned advanced reading material versus those who are not, and students assigned higher level work are often perceived as being given more challenging tasks or work in addition to that which the other students are completing. Conversely, students may be told that they have to complete lower level work because they are not doing well; students can give examples of being told that they were performing at levels below those of their peers. Students also glean ideas about whether they are being successful or not from the degree of teacher monitoring. Teachers are perceived to give those considered smart a lot of independence whereas those who are not doing as well are much more closely monitored. Students acknowledge that some of these differences arise because the teacher wants to help those achieving at lower levels. However, those students for whom teachers have lower expectations may miss out on some activities; they may have to complete work during recess or while the others engage in physical education. Students report that this does not happen to high achievers.

Assessment of work. The feedback that students receive on their work also gives them information about their teachers' expectations of them. This may be direct or indirect. For example, students report that teachers mostly call on high expectation students, or on those from the top ability group. They also interpret smiley or sad faces on their work as showing whether or not they have done well. These more subtle teacher messages are more meaningful to students than marks or grades on the same piece of work. Further, even the feedback that indicates to students that they will probably do better next time, is an indication that they are not currently doing well. Students also report the shame that can be felt when teachers make fun of some students for not doing well.

Motivation of students. Students report being motivated by extrinsic rewards such as treats and small gifts. They also express a sense of pride when they receive a reward from the teacher.

Nevertheless, students are also mindful that effort can result in improved performance. Some students spoke of encouraging teachers who gave them a sense of self-belief that they could improve, of working harder, and of succeeding. Reasons that students give for the failure of low achievers is that they do not try hard enough, that they do not like schoolwork, that they misbehave in class, and that do not complete the set work. However, students also explained that low achievers lacked motivation because they were often yelled at by teachers and because they were given boring tasks to complete.

Student autonomy. In some classrooms, students are given very little autonomy; most interactions are teacher-initiated and most decisions are made by the teacher. However, students do perceive that teachers often give high expectation students independent work and they are left alone to complete it. Students describe how this sense of teacher trust imbues them with a sense of responsibility to work on their own and complete their work within the required timeframe. On the other hand, students describe how some teachers keep a much closer watch on those considered low achievers; they are monitored much more closely and not given either independence or choice about their learning activities. Students also perceive that high achievers become peer tutors when they complete their work early and also that these are the students who complete errands for the teacher.

Classroom relationships. Teachers set the tone for the relationships in the classroom. In situations where all students feel accepted and there are not high levels of discrimination in the ways that students are treated, students are likely to be more supportive of other students. In classrooms where the tone becomes more divisive, both the high achievers and the lows can be teased by other students, one group for being nerds or such like, the other for not being smart. Students report that teachers often favor those they expect more from in comparison to those they expect less from. Some of these differences epitomize those described by Elisha Babad whereby he reported that teachers favor high expectation students emotionally. This favoritism is perceived by students in a number of ways. For example, teachers are described as being warmer towards high achievers. This can be reflected in facial expressions as reported by students, but can also be evident in teachers forming more personal relationships with those perceived to be smart. Teachers may joke with or tease (in a nice way) students for whom their expectations are higher. They are also described by students as showing trust in high expectation students but not in lows. They are trusted to do the "right thing," to complete work to a high standard, and to remain engaged. On the other hand, students report that teachers are more vigilant with low achievers. Teachers show they are concerned about the progress of lows but this tends to be displayed in a more business-like manner without the warmth accorded the highs.

Students are also aware of the privileges accorded highs in the wider school environment. For example, students report that high achievers are chosen to complete errands or tasks that need completing at the school-level. Other students are never offered these opportunities. High achievers might create posters for a school fair. Students are aware that those considered smart are allowed to do these tasks because they complete work early, but, nevertheless, students consider the differential treatment to be unfair. High expectation students also seem to be selected more frequently to represent the school in extracurricular activities, and, at times, they are selected to go on field trips that the other students are precluded from.

INTERVIEWS WITH STUDENTS

Interviews by Weinstein and her colleagues with fourth and fifth graders enabled in-depth exploration of teacher messages about smartness.[22] Students reported that they learn whether they are considered smart or not mostly from the teacher and not so much from their peers or their families. Students said that their teachers often provide feedback that tells them whether the teacher considers they are smart or not. These remarks are frequently comparative. For example, the teacher might refer to her best mathematicians, and because students are generally in ability groups, they know whether or not they are in that elite group. On the other hand, the teacher may refer to students who need lots of help.

Students can also detail other teacher verbal and nonverbal behavior, for example, a teacher showing they are angry when a student is having difficulty, perhaps by yelling at a particular student or even by the way that a teacher glares at the student or rolls their eyes. Sadly, many students are able to report times that they or their peers have been mocked or humiliated by their teachers when they have struggled to complete some work. This harks back to the critical incidents that I spoke of earlier; one cutting remark that stays with a child for a very long time and can influence their future academic trajectory.

One consistent factor is that these references to student smartness are often public, and so children are shamed or glorified in front of all their classmates. Similarly, students report that only certain students are asked to respond to teacher questions, and they believe that it is always those the teacher thinks will know the correct answer. Those students for whom teachers have low expectations are only asked questions when they are not paying attention, and students report that the teacher asks them then so that they will stop misbehaving or being distracted and become engaged in the class work. When students were asked how they can get smart, interestingly, they reported that this related to student behavior. For example, students associated smartness with paying attention and sitting quietly. They also associated it with being able to complete work quickly and easily, and with getting it right.

Perhaps not surprisingly, students can depict the emotions they have experienced when they have felt unsuccessful because of a teacher comment or nonverbal behavior (such as the teacher rolling her eyes). Students report feeling physically ill or very hurt by a teacher comment or action. Some also report losing motivation, of giving up trying when it seems nothing they do warrants praise. On the other hand, a few take the teacher comments on board and resolve to try harder and to do better. Teacher praise or a kind word bring about very different emotions. Students feel a sense of pride when they are told they have done well; praise can be motivating. However, when students are in ability groups, then they express anxiety about being moved down to a lower group if they do not perform and, therefore, the pressure of having to maintain high performance.

A DIFFERENT CONTEXT

The careful and thorough work of Rhona Weinstein has not been replicated elsewhere and so it is unknown whether the lives that students have reported living in classrooms and that she has so carefully described[22] are more universally experienced. Half a world away, in New Zealand, one of my doctoral students, Nane Rio,[23] recently conducted a study where she administered the Teacher Treatment Inventory,[24,25] which Weinstein developed to capture students' perceptions of how high and low expectation students experience their classroom lives. Rio also interviewed 50 randomly chosen students about how they knew whether they were smart or not. The study provides an interesting contrast to the findings of Weinstein because the research was conducted in both a provincial and urban setting and included a large number of students (over 1000). In the following section, I will report the findings of Rio by providing a summary of some of the findings from the questionnaires as well as illustrative quotes from students that poignantly reflect what Weinstein has found. The study by Rio is important because it seems to show that many of the behaviors students identified in Weinstein's studies were also reported in New Zealand classrooms, and therefore can be assumed to be more ubiquitous than isolated to one area of the United States.

Students reported that teachers had low expectations for low achievers, particularly boys. They also believed that teachers gave high achievers more independence but monitored low achievers more closely. Coupled with this, low achievers were viewed as being treated more negatively by teachers whereas high achievers were the subject of teacher support not accorded the low achievers. Similarly, high achievers were perceived as being more popular, friendly, competitive, focused, independent, successful, and more likely to possess leadership qualities than those not considered smart by the teacher.

The student comments from the interviews were grouped into three key areas: Messages students received from the teacher that told them whether or not they were smart, the different instructional environment that high and low achieving students experienced, and how students would treat others if they were the teacher.

Teacher messages about smartness. Students reported being given both verbal and nonverbal messages from teachers that let them know whether they were considered smart or not. From a student achieving well: "[The teacher] congratulate me [sic] ... they push me to the best of my ability ... [and] use your work as like an example to show somebody else." Teachers also gave nonverbal signals that indicated whether or not students were doing well: "Like impressions ... facial expressions, they smile at you."

The type of work that students received and the ways in which the teacher interacted with students also indicated how smart the teacher believed students were: "[The teacher] helps them [low achieving students] with their work . . . makes it easier for them." Similarly to Weinstein's work, students in New Zealand also shared that teachers were more vigilant towards the low achievers and at times appeared to hurt their feelings:

> [The teacher would] always look up to see if we are doing the work . . . the teacher tells us the answer . . . [or] gets one of the smarter children to work with them . . . if she gets frustrated with that person then the teacher would, umm, get another person to try and teach that person as well. They shame them out in front of the class.

At times it seemed that other adults might also be enlisted to work with low achievers. Again, students readily understood what this meant in terms of who was considered smart: "Every time a helper [teacher aide] comes into the class, the teacher will take the smart people . . . The others that need help will go to the helper." Students also interpreted what teachers said as an indication of whether they were considered smart of not: "[The teacher] says good job, but you need to improve." On the other hand, students considered smart, received only favorable recognition from teachers.

Overall, as found in the United States, students in New Zealand had very clearly defined views about how many teachers treated very differently those perceived to be smart or not. At times the descriptions of the students revealed quite subtle distinctions and not achievement differences deliberately pointed out by teachers, but students interpreted the messages and had a perceptive understanding of how they were doing as a result of an array of teacher behaviors.

The instructional environment. Reminiscent of some of the findings of Rhona Weinstein, the students in this New Zealand study also associated engagement and task completion as indicative of smartness. High achievers were described as: "Get high marks ... good report ... they know their stuff ... a student that is brainy [smart] is on task and finishes off his work quickly ... they don't muck around ... and they do their hard work [sic]." Students had quite different views of low achievers: "Get low marks ... students who are not brainy get a not-so-good report ... mucks around and plays instead of doing his work."

High expectation students were those who teachers called on:

> [There are] always a couple of people putting their hands up. You can tell they are really onto it ... the brainy ones, they answer all the questions ... if the teacher asks a question and if someone gets it wrong and the other gets it right you can usually tell how he or she explains [whether they are smart or not] ... they are better at explaining things.

The students appeared to be aware that the low achievers were not asked to respond to questions as often as the high achievers.

Within class ability groups were a salient reminder of students' positions in the class: "The not-so-brainy students go into the medium or lower group than the highest group [sic] ... and they hardly do their work and just sit there and don't answer questions ... lower groups are full of the kids that need to improve." In contrast: "The brainy people they don't get told off by the teacher ... the smarter groups are full of the brainy students."

Students were asked how some students became smart. Most believed that you became smart through effort: " ... by paying attention in the class and understanding what to do and always trying even though you don't know because you learn from that ... they study hard." And, in order to become smart, student effort went beyond the classroom:

> You read rather than play or watch TV; you get used to this and be smart [sic] . . . they study hard, they go like, night time instead of watching TV, watching all those movies, they go into bed with a torch light or something and then they read stories and they understand it, like they imagine it in their brain what the story is about [sic]. They come to school the next day; they think about what they did last night.

However, a few did think that high achievers were born that way and that having supportive parents helped: "Probably they grow up with brainy dads . . . yeah, just grow up with a brainy dad and mom . . . ummm, some people are like natural at it."

Students also had views about whether students continued achieving at high levels throughout their schooling. Generally they agreed, provided students continued to put in effort:

> When they listen and do not muck around and do not hang around with the bad people . . . by being resilient and trying harder . . . if they push themselves and give themselves a goal for next year, I reckon they will be brainy.

Some students gave more direct responses about whether students would continue to achieve highly in subsequent years: "[Yes] because you don't lose your brains over one year . . . yeah, they are still brainy next year because they just know it, like it's stuck in their brain pretty much."

Students associated high achievers with learning concepts easily and with always getting answers correct. Generally it was thought that smart students enjoyed school and that they were popular among other students. However, this was not always the perception: "Most brainy children are usually quiet because sometimes they get bullied." Nevertheless, students perceived that high achievers garnered a special place in school: "The

Expectations, Interactions, and Perceptions

school thinks of you higher; they expect more." On the other hand, most students believed that low achievers had a much harder time at school than high achievers:

> They need a lot of help. It's hard and they always have to try hard to get up to a higher level . . . They might be a bit put down by the teacher and they might not be learning. It's quite hard for them cause, like, when someone asks you something and you don't know, others laugh at you.

Low achievers were also perceived as being disruptive. Interestingly, this was attributed to boredom: "Like they play and that in class . . . they are bored . . . really social and really loud. They always talk and fight with each other." However, the reported differential behavior of low and high achievers did not seem to be evident in every classroom. One student was positive about low achievers: "Yeah, they are nice . . . they're good looking . . . quiet, fairly quiet and they just get on with stuff." This same child went on to say:

> Well, my class, we are a mixed class cause we've got the higher students but we all act the same. We don't really have very many fights very often, like between friends. We don't make fun of each other or anything. We are a pretty good class.

In most classes, students seemed to be aware of the students who teachers expected to do well. They were students who learned easily and who did not struggle. High achievers were also perceived as being better behaved than low achievers. There was evidence from students that both high and low achievers could be bullied by others. Generally students thought that students who were doing well would continue in that vein provided they continued to put in effort. Interestingly, although high achievers

Expectations, Interactions, and Perceptions 57

were perceived by students as learning easily, they were also thought of as putting in additional effort, not just at school, but also at home, by torchlight!

The student as the teacher. Students were asked what they would do if they were the teacher, that is, how they would treat students. Their responses are presented below:

> I would always work with the people that are not brainy . . . I would make the work easier for them but still make it a little bit hard and then make it harder each time they do their work. I will help them and I won't give up on the kids and I will work my hardest. I would show them how to work out an answer or how to look for things, and making sure that they're doing their work so that they learn more and be more smart [sic] . . . would teach them as much as possible. If I can't, I will get the smart children to help them . . . I'll make sure they do more reading and writing with them, and if they improve more I'll make them go to a higher level and I would keep helping them and encouraging them to do better, I'll tell the parents to help them more at home with their reading or something   probably like make groups . . . and like make the not-so-brainy people like do kinda easier work to start, and then just get them onto harder stuff so they can learn.

Another student seemed to think that teachers needed to be more adaptable to student needs: "Well, I'd just find an easier way that they could understand it instead of the way that you [the teacher] understand it. You gotta find ways so that they can understand it."

The views of the students in this New Zealand study are remarkably similar to those of the student views reported by Weinstein.[22] I began this chapter by illustrating how teachers portray their expectations through their differential behaviors. The chapter then focused on the student perspectives, not only providing findings from other studies but also presenting students' voices, their lived experiences. Overwhelmingly, it seems that many teachers differentiate in the ways in which they treat those perceived to be high or low achievers. Moreover, students notice these differences and from the ways that teachers treat students, they come to view themselves as a learner and to develop understandings that inform their ideas about their capabilities. Although some of the teacher behaviors may be strongly argued by some as necessary to enhance student learning, the reports by students of teacher criticism, humiliation, and frustration cannot be justified. There are also a growing body of academics and teaching professionals who are coming to recognize the detrimental effects to students of frequently making ability salient in classrooms, particularly through ability grouping. The differentiation of learning that results is most likely not helped by the punitive assessment schedule demanded of students and teachers. It must often seem that no sooner is one examination out of the way but another is looming. This can lead to further differentiation in what students are taught and learn.

So, what have we learned in this chapter? In this chapter, differential teacher behaviors have been reported by teachers themselves, by classroom observers and by the students. Teachers do seem to have lower expectations of some students than of others and this is reflected in teacher actions, verbal behavior, and nonverbal behavior in many classrooms. Students notice this and report how the differential teacher behaviors in some classrooms make them feel. Teachers are the professionals in the student-teacher relationship. It is up to them to dispense their praise, their warmth, and their care equitably among all students regardless of achievement level. Students notice and respond accordingly. Many teachers provide wonderful learning environments for their students. Students notice and respond accordingly – they flourish in classrooms where they feel supported and cared for.

Although equitable treatment of students and equitable learning opportunities are an ultimate goal for education, there is a history of some students being given more opportunities to learn than others. The next chapter will consider a wide range of student characteristics that can make them more vulnerable to teachers' expectations.

REFERENCES

1. Brophy JE, Good TL. Teacher-child dyadic interaction system. *Mirrors for Behaviour: An Anthology of Observation Instruments continued*. Vol A. Philadelphia: Research for Better Schools, Inc; 1970.
2. Brophy JE, Good TL. Teachers' communication of differential expectations for children's classroom performance: Some behavioral data. *Journal of Educational Psychology*. 1970;61:365–374.
3. Brophy JE, Good TL. *Teacher-student relationships: Causes and consequences*. New York: Holt, Rinehart & Winston; 1974.
4. Good T. Which pupils do teachers call on? *Elementary School Journal*. 1970;70:190–198.
5. Brophy JE. Research on the self-fulfilling prophecy and teacher expectations. *Journal of Educational Psychology*. 1983;75:631–661.
6. Brophy JE. Teacher-student interaction. In: Dusek JB, ed. *Teacher expectancies*. Hillsdale: Lawrence Erlbaum; 1985:303–328.
7. Rist RC. Student social class and teacher expectations: The self-fulfilling prophecy in ghetto education. *Harvard Educational Review*. 1970;40:411–451.
8. Babad E. Preferential affect: The crux of the teacher expectancy issue. In: Brophy J, ed. *Advances in research on teaching: Expectations in the classroom*. Vol 7. Greenwich: JAI Press; 1998:183–214.
9. Babad E. The final word. In: Rubie-Davies CM, Stephens JM, Watson P, eds. *Routledge international handbook of social psychology of the classroom*. London: Routledge; 2015:385–394.
10. Harris MJ, Rosenthal R. Mediation of interpersonal expectancy effects: 31 meta-analyses. *Psychological Bulletin*. 1985;97:363–386.
11. Babad E. *The social psychology of the classroom*. New York: Routledge; 2009.
12. Zohar A, Degani A, Vaaknin E. Teachers' beliefs about low-achieving students and higher order thinking. *Teaching and Teacher Education*. 2001;17:469–485.
13. Rubie-Davies CM. *Becoming a high expectation teacher: Raising the bar*. London: Routledge; 2015.

Expectations, Interactions, and Perceptions

14. Babad E. Measuring and changing teachers' differential behavior as perceived by students and teachers. *Journal of Educational Psychology.* 1990;82:683–690.
15. Babad E. The "teacher's pet" phenomenon, teachers' differential behavior, and students' morale. *Journal of Educational Psychology.* 1995;87:361–374.
16. Babad E, Bernieri F, Rosenthal R. When less information is more informative: Diagnosing teacher expectations from brief samples of behaviour. *British Journal of Educational Psychology.* 1989;59:281–295.
17. Babad E, Bernieri F, Rosenthal R. Students as judges of teachers' verbal and nonverbal behavior. *American Educational Research Journal.* 1991;28:211–234.
18. Babad E, Taylor PB. Transparency of teacher expectancies across language, cultural boundaries. *Journal of Educational Research.* 1992;86:120–125.
19. Pianta RC, Belsky J, Vandergrift N, Houts R, Morrison FJ. Classroom effects on children's achievement trajectories in elementary school. *American Educational Research Journal.* 2008;45:365–397.
20. Pianta RC, Hamre BK, Allen JP. Teacher-student relationships and engagement: Conceptualizing, measuring, and improving the capacity of classroom interactions. In: Christenson SL, Reschly AL, Wylie C, eds. *Handbook of research on student engagement.* New York: Springer 2012.
21. Pianta RC, Stuhlman MW. Teacher-child relationships and children's success in the first years of school. *School Psychology Review.* 2004;33:444–458.
22. Weinstein RS. *Reaching higher: The power of expectations in schooling.* Cambridge: Harvard University Press; 2002.
23. Rio NT. *Teacher expectations and ethnicity: Student and teacher perspectives.* Unpublished doctoral thesis, Auckland, The University of Auckland; 2017.
24. Weinstein RS, Marshall HH, Sharp L, Botkin M. Pygmalion and the student: Age and classroom differences in children's awareness of teacher expectations. *Child Development.* 1987;58:1079–1093.
25. Weinstein RS, Middlestadt SE. Student perceptions of teacher interactions with male high and low achievers. *Journal of Educational Psychology.* 1979;71:421–431.

Three
Student Characteristics as Precursors to Differential Teacher Expectations

In the first chapter, I described the seminal work in the teacher expectation field, Pygmalion. I also explained some of the political and social context that contributed to a background for the study, the fact that children of poverty had little chance of success within the education system, the civil unrest of the 1960s, and the deeply ingrained racism towards African Americans. Because Pygmalion appeared to show that positively-biased teacher expectations could influence student outcomes, questions arose as to whether or not low teacher expectations could have negative influences on student outcomes. Given the political situation, whether student characteristics could influence teachers' expectations negatively, and, in turn, affect student outcomes became of interest. Questions began to be asked such as, do teachers form differential expectations for different types of students? If student characteristics lead teachers to form low expectations for some students and high for others, what stereotypes, criteria, or information might teachers use when developing their expectations?

Over many years now, a host of student characteristics have been explored as potentially influencing teacher expectations. Most of the focus in this area has been on exploring teacher expectations in relation to ethnicity, socioeconomic status, gender, and student labelling. However, many other student characteristics have also been explored, including the influence of giftedness, student language, names, family circumstances, and student personality factors.

Although not strictly a student characteristic per se, the portfolio information that teachers are given for each child can influence teachers' expectations for their students, at times before they have even met the students. Some teachers studiously read all the information that they receive on each student before the school year begins. Unfortunately, this can bias teachers' perceptions. They form expectations for some students at that point. I was once on a research project investigating how teachers set up their classrooms for the new academic year and was surprised to find that many teachers had placed students into within-class ability groups in reading and mathematics before the year had even begun. Those who spent time with their students before making any decisions about appropriate learning experiences were actually in the minority. I was shocked because, in most classes, the students were labeled before the year had even begun. Hence, both formal portfolio information and informal teacher comments about students passed on from teacher to teacher are strong predictors of teachers' expectations. Nevertheless, a huge focus of teacher expectation research has aimed to explore how specific student characteristics become precursors to teachers' expectations. In the remainder of this chapter, I will be discussing student characteristics and how they can both positively and negatively bias teacher expectations. I will begin by talking about the big four: Ethnicity, social class, gender, and labeling students as having special needs of some sort. These are the four student characteristics that have most often been investigated and which most is known about. The remainder have been explored in fewer studies but nevertheless have interesting findings.

ETHNICITY

Most Western societies are diverse. Many accommodate what can be termed "voluntary minorities" (those who have moved from another country to their new host country), for example,

Turkish students in Germany, and some include minorities who are either indigenous, for example, Inuit Indians in Canada, or who were forced to live in a particular country at some time in history, for example, African Americans. In almost all Western countries, minority groups such as those listed above achieve at levels lower than those of their majority peers. Education is seen as a vehicle by which minority groups can gain the privileges of the White middle class; immigrant parents often cite getting a better education for their children as one motivator for moving to a new country. However, if education is to enable everyone to succeed, then the system needs to be fair and should provide equal opportunities for all. Unfortunately, this is often not the case. Minority students may be offered a curriculum that does not enable them to move into college later in their educational career. This may be due to tracking or simply that the schools they attend do not offer the curriculum needed in order to advance to college. Minority students may not have the best teachers in front of them. In some systems, teachers working in low socioeconomic communities are paid less than their counterparts working in middle class areas. Minority group students may have parents unfamiliar with the education system and who are unsure how to negotiate it either because they left school early themselves or if they are immigrant parents, they may not understand the system in their new country as well as those born in the host country. Whatever the explanation, teacher expectations have often been seen as one vehicle by which students' life chances might be restricted.

There is a long history of the examination of teacher expectations of minority groups and whether or not these affect students. Mostly, the evidence does point to minority status as biasing teachers' expectations negatively[1] but there has been the occasional exception, mostly in European studies[2], where minority students have received higher expectations from teachers than the majority. Nevertheless, a mostly consistent pattern is the finding that expectations tend to be lower for ethnic minority groups, even when achievement is taken into account.[1–3] Depending on the context, expectations are lower for different groups.

The United States. In the United States, expectations tend to be lower for African American,[1] Hispanic,[4] Appalachian,[5] and Native American students.[6] Further, although they tend to be more successful in school than other minority groups, Asian students have experienced discrimination when entering some high schools, and particularly at the university level[7] where they may be refused entry to prestigious colleges even though they meet the required standards.

Several studies have shown that even when there is no difference in student achievement, teachers have lower expectations for African American students than they do for White students.[4, 8] More recently, a synthesis of several studies[1] of the effects of ethnicity on teacher expectations showed that teachers did favor White students over both African American and Latino/a students. Across several studies, it was also shown that teachers were more positive in their interactions with White students than they were with the other two groups. Although investigated less frequently, as with African American students, teacher expectations also tend to be lower for Latino/a students than for white students.[4] Further, teachers may rate ethnic minority students lower on a range of characteristics. For example, Latino/a students have been rated lower for learning, motivational, creativity, and leadership characteristics than White students.[9] Further, teachers tend to have higher expectations for Latino/a students that they judge to be more acculturated than they do for their counterparts who are more recent immigrants.[9] In the United States, Native Americans and Appalachians[5, 6] may also be the subject of low teacher expectations. It is thought that because Native Americans tend to achieve at fairly low levels and have high dropout rates, that it is likely that teachers would generalize low expectations to all members of the Native American group without careful consideration of individuals. Similarly, because of the cultural isolation of Appalachians and their particular dialect, there is a perception that they lack intelligence. Again, this is likely to lead to low teacher expectations.

Canada. In Canada, expectations for Canadian Native Indians have been found to be lower than for White Canadians.[10,11] In an experimental study,[10] preservice teachers were given descriptions of students and their achievement. Half the descriptions were ascribed to Native Canadians whereas the other half supposedly pertained to White students. The preservice teachers then made placement recommendations for the students. Even though the descriptions of the fictitious students did not vary, the preservice teachers consistently recommended lower placements for the Native Canadian students. Practicing teachers have also been found to be biased and to similarly recommend Native Canadian students for remedial programs even when grades do not indicate remedial assignment should be considered.[11] Interestingly, however, teachers assigned high achieving Native Canadians correctly. They reported that this was because they noticed such students when they did well because they did not expect them to be achieving at high levels.

Israel. In Israel, findings are similar.[12] Psychology students were given an essay supposedly written by either a gifted or remedial Israeli versus Moroccan student. The differences in grades assigned to the remedial versus the gifted Israeli student were not nearly as large as the differences in grades assigned to gifted versus remedial Moroccan students. So, it seems that when students come from a low status group and yet achieve at high levels, teachers may pay more attention to them and, hopefully encourage and support them more than their White peers. On the other hand, those achieving at lower levels are likely to be subjected to even lower expectations than they deserve and consequent reduced opportunities to learn.

United Kingdom. The United Kingdom, and specifically England, has a very diverse population. This is partly the result of the British Empire when many countries were colonies of Great Britain and therefore the citizens of those various countries were entitled to live and work in the United Kingdom. The diversity of the population is also the result of Britain's former membership of the European Union which meant that anyone whose country was also a member could immigrate to the United Kingdom, if they so wished.

In the 1950s and 1960s, as in some other Western countries, overt racism signals were ever-present in the United Kingdom. Blacks and people of color were barred from many venues such as shops and restaurants. Those overt signs have long gone, and it might be hoped that racist attitudes have similarly declined. Hence, it is interesting to reflect on the fact that a central focus of the 2010 General Election was anti-immigrant policy, resulting in stricter language tests for new immigrants, and very recently England's exit from the European Union appears to have been racially based. It is perhaps not surprising then that teacher expectations for some students in the United Kingdom appear to suggest teacher bias.

Pakistani students are one group for whom teachers appear to have low expectations.[13,14] In one school, Pakistani students were achieving at lower levels than White students.[14] Teachers explained that this was partly because the parents showed that they were not interested in their children's education by not attending parent interviews. When the parents were approached, it was found that school notices were sent home in English and many of the Pakistani parents did not speak English. Once the newsletters were translated, there was an immediate increase in parental attendance at interviews. One teacher of the younger students sent reading books home with her students so that they could practice with their parents. However, she did not allow Pakistani students to take books home. The teacher argued that the students would not read the books anyway nor would they return them. Thus, the students' opportunities to learn were being constrained. Such views appear to be pervasive because interviews in a different part of the country also revealed low teacher expectations for both Pakistani and Bangladeshi students.[13] Again, teachers reported that parent aspirations for their children were low, especially for girls, but when parents were interviewed, they expressed aspirations that their children would go to university, and they had similarly high aspirations for both genders.

Another group for whom teachers in the United Kingdom have been reported to have low expectations are Afro-Caribbean students.[15] Even when achievement is controlled, at the secondary school level, Afro-Caribbean students are less likely to be recommended for higher tier (more advanced) mathematics and science tests which would enable them to take courses in those fields at university. For every three White students with the same achievement as their Afro-Caribbean peers who complete higher tier tests, only two Afro-Caribbean students are allowed to sit the same tests. It is also interesting to note that, overall, the gap between Afro-Caribbean and White students is largest in mathematics and science, curriculum areas which have tiered tests, and much smaller in English, which does not have tiered tests. Entry into a tiered testing system makes teacher expectations explicit to students and may have demotivating effects on Afro-Caribbean students achieving at high levels but not recommended for the higher tier. Placement in lower tiers also has the long-term effect of potentially limiting students' opportunities for higher education.

Even for Afro-Caribbean and other Black students who succeed in education and enter middle class occupations, this does not seem to immunize their children from low teacher expectations and what can only be described as racism and racist attitudes.[16] Parents described being called racist names by teachers when they were at school or, when they were successful, having to endure teacher surprise. For example, one parent described being refused entry to the school chess club initially, and then when winning against the top player in a rival school, having a teacher express surprise that a Black student could play chess, let alone win. And even though a generation had passed, these same parents found that they were constantly having to deal with teachers' low expectations for their own children. Parents could detail instances of their children achieving highly but never receiving school prizes or of being passed over for gifted and talented programs when they clearly should have been considered. Parents also reported times when teachers had openly expressed expectations that a Black student should not anticipate more than a bare pass in examinations even though some students were highly capable. One such student later received several of the very highest passes in an external examination and, other than one subject, all passes were As.

Western Europe. Immigration within Western European nations also accelerated following World War II and has continued. There are now large Turkish populations, for example, in both Germany and the Netherlands. However, the evidence for teacher expectations being biased by ethnicity is less conclusive in European countries than in the findings from countries described above. The track that teachers recommended students be placed in following elementary school has been used as a measure of teachers' expectations for their students. In other words, track recommendation was compared with student achievement in order to determine whether the teacher recommendation was accurate, too high or too low. In Germany, teacher expectations for Turkish students have been shown to be biased[17] with teachers expecting less of Turkish students than German students. But it may be that teacher expectations for Turkish students are simply less accurate because teachers have also been shown to overestimate high achieving Turkish students compared to German students.[18] Nevertheless, recommending a student for a higher track than current achievement suggests may be less detrimental to the students' long-term prospects than recommending that a student be placed in a low track when their achievement data shows that a higher track would be more appropriate.

In the Netherlands, the evidence of low expectations for ethnic minority students is similarly mixed.[2, 19] Generally teachers' expectations in the Netherlands are not shown to be biased by ethnicity, again using track recommendation as a proxy for expectations. However, in the Netherlands, student characteristics other than ethnicity may influence teacher expectations. One of these is socioeconomic status, which will be discussed in the next section.

Australia. There does seem to be some evidence of ethnic bias in teacher expectations in Australia. Among both preservice and practicing teachers, expectations were found to reflect societal stereotypes.[20] That is, both preservice and practicing teachers had higher expectations for Anglo-Australian and Asian students than for Aboriginal students in both mathematics and English. Aboriginal students were also rated lower for talent and effort and were the only group to be consistently rated below average on all scales. Further, in line with stereotypical perceptions, teachers also believed that Aboriginal students' families were less supportive of their educational career, Asian parents were perceived to be most supportive, and Anglo-Australian support from families fell in the middle. Also reflecting stereotypes, whereas expectations for Asian students were higher in mathematics, they were higher for Anglo-Australian students in English. Similar patterns have been found in New Zealand, although there does appear to be some shift latterly in teacher expectations in that country.

New Zealand. New Zealand is a very multi-ethnic society but the various groups are generally categorized into four main clusters: New Zealand European, Māori (the indigenous group), Pasifika (those originating from one of the Pacific Islands (e.g., Samoa, Tonga, Fiji, Niue), and Asian (those from South East Asia and the Indian subcontinent). About 10 years ago, at both elementary[3] and secondary[21] levels, teacher expectations appeared to be lower for Māori than for any other group. What was interesting about this was that expectations for Pasifika students were higher than they were for Māori and yet the achievement of Pasifika students was lower than that of any other group. The prevailing stereotype appeared to be that Pasifika parents were more supportive of their children's education than were Māori families. However, although there do seem to be some teachers, particularly at secondary level, who have openly expressed negative expectations towards Māori very recently,[22] there is some evidence that explicit expectations are beginning to become more positive for Māori.

So, what has changed? There are some possible explanations. The Ministry of Education have had a major focus on trying to raise teacher expectations, particularly for groups like Māori and Pasifika students. Schools have to show how they are lifting the achievement of both minority groups in line with higher expectations from the government. Further, two large teacher expectation and professional development projects, one at elementary level[23] and one at secondary,[24] have shown that changed teacher practices focused on raising expectations and implementing culturally responsive practices can significantly lift the achievement of Māori and Pasifika students. It may be that these initiatives have contributed to changes in teachers' expectations. Of course, if you are a cynic you may believe that teachers have simply learned to hide their true expectations!

When teachers' explicit expectations have been measured more recently, no evidence of teacher bias has been found among two separate and large samples of students in elementary[25] and middle schools,[26] when achievement has been taken into account. Instead, implicit bias has been found.[25] So, although professional development and Ministry of Education initiatives may have contributed to teacher adjustment of their explicit expectations, teachers do still appear to be subject to stereotyping, and this can affect student achievement.

A way forward. The biasing of teacher expectations by ethnicity is probably the most contentious of all student characteristics in terms of the idea that ethnicity might influence teacher expectations. From a social justice perspective, ethnicity should have no influence on teacher expectations; the only criterion should be student achievement. The idea that ethnicity does affect teacher expectations implies that teachers do not provide educational opportunities equally to all students. Some are being advantaged whereas others are not. The findings further suggest that teachers may be contributing to some of the societal disparities found in most Western nations. Most teachers would find this idea repugnant. Unfortunately, in repeated studies, biases have been found. How might these be overcome? The New Zealand context is interesting because teachers' explicit expectations, at least, have shown a shift. This suggests that, given appropriate professional development, teachers do alter their expectations for minority groups. Any professional development needs a focus on high expectations and how those expectations should be translated into classrooms, as well as a focus on culturally responsive pedagogy – teachers working with students in ways that are respectful and caring of students, and likely to lead to increased achievement. Often expectations are portrayed nonverbally so a further

72 **Student Characteristics**

suggestion is that teachers video their own practice and then self-analyze their behavior. Implicit bias, which is often unconscious, can also be measured online and without scrutiny: www.understandingprejudice.org/iat/. Measurement of personal bias provides a platform for further development.

This section of the chapter on ethnicity has been expansive. This is partly because ethnicity has been investigated most often in terms of student characteristics that can influence teacher expectations, but also because it is the most controversial. Another student characteristic that has been investigated fairly often is student social class. Again, the many studies in the field seem to show that socioeconomic status can affect teacher expectations. Remembering back to the first chapter, the study by Rist[27] appeared to show that student social class could influence teacher expectations leading teachers to provide differential opportunities to learn for those from middle versus low socioeconomic circumstances. This is the focus for the next section of this chapter.

SOCIAL CLASS

Interestingly, social class as a precursor to teacher expectations has been investigated less frequently than ethnicity but the findings are far more straightforward: In the vast majority of studies, social class or socioeconomic status does appear to influence teacher expectations. As far back as 1972,[28] there were measurements of teachers' expectations in relation to social class. By the mid-1980s there were several studies in the United States that had tried to determine whether or not social class influenced teacher expectations and a synthesis[29] of all of the studies at the time concluded that, indeed, teacher expectations were influenced by social class. Similar results were also found overseas.[30] So, collectively, the evidence pointed to a lowering of teacher expectations when students came from low socioeconomic backgrounds and an inflation of expectations when students came from middle class homes.

Student and teacher factors. The quest then became to explore various factors that might be contributing to lowered teacher expectations for those from low socioeconomic backgrounds. Student factors are one consideration. That is, student behavior and motivation may contribute to teacher expectations. However, even when those factors are taken into account, teachers still tend to underestimate students from low socioeconomic backgrounds and overestimate middle class students.[31] Further, at the class rather than the individual level, even when the achievement of students in middle class and low socioeconomic classrooms is the same, teachers tend to assign higher grades to students in middle class classrooms and to grade students in low socioeconomic status classrooms more harshly. Interestingly, teacher socioeconomic background does not seem to play a role in moderating expectations. That is, even when teachers have reported that at 16 years of age their family was of low socioeconomic status,[31] they have still differentiated in their judgments of students from low or high socioeconomic backgrounds.

Levels of teacher training and teaching experience do not appear to influence teacher expectations although the findings are mixed with some studies finding that more advanced degrees and greater levels of teacher experience do contribute to teacher expectations but other studies finding no differences.[32] Further studies will be needed to unravel the contribution of teacher factors to their expectations. However, what is evident is that less experienced and less qualified teachers are more often found in low socioeconomic areas, and these teachers tend to have less favorable views of their students' academic capabilities. At the class level, young students have better reading achievement when they are in classes where the instructional practices vary, where there are plenty of teaching resources, where there are fewer students in the class, and where there are fewer students reading at below average levels. However, students from low socioeconomic backgrounds seem to benefit most from lower class numbers. Students from these groups tend to get lower reading scores when they are in large classes and better scores when they are in classes that are smaller than average. These findings are not replicated in high socioeconomic status classrooms where no association is revealed between class size and student outcomes.[32] This suggests that one way in which the achievement of students from low socioeconomic backgrounds might be increased would be to reduce class sizes in schools situated in poorer communities. Reduced class sizes in those areas may also provide an incentive for teachers to opt for employment in schools in lower social class neighborhoods, providing a wider pool of quality teachers to select from. In turn, this could improve teacher quality in those schools.

Differentiation, ability grouping, and tracking. Teachers can also constrain or promote student learning depending on the opportunities provided for student learning. It does seem that both educational systems and teacher actions can serve to limit the opportunities for students from low socioeconomic communities. For example, students in a low socioeconomic school were achieving well below the national mean at Grade 2.[33] The school wanted to investigate why this was happening and whether or not the achievement could be turned around. The researchers found that Kindergarten teachers were delaying the teaching of reading because their perception was that the students needed a number of pre-reading skills before formal teaching could begin. Hence, the teachers spent the first year of students' schooling ensuring that the students had the pre-reading skills which were precursory to learning to read. Formal teaching of reading began in students' second year. The next 40 entering students were then tested on the pre-reading skills.

Overall, the students already had 80 percent of the skills when they arrived at school – skills that the teachers were spending a full academic year teaching. Once this was recognized and the teachers began teaching reading immediately on student entry, within three years, all students in the school were achieving at national levels.

These findings show how, at the very beginning of schooling, students can be set on a particular academic trajectory which tends to be maintained throughout students' school life, unless there is some form of intervention. Factors that can contribute to or exacerbate student opportunities for equitable outcomes and life chances for students from low socioeconomic backgrounds include ability grouping and tracking. Although the proportion of schools that track in the United States is purported to have reduced,[34] nevertheless among those who admit to tracking in their schools, the percentage of low socioeconomic status students in any school, predicts the tracks that are offered. For example, among schools in low socioeconomic areas, vocational education is likely to be the dominant offering whereas in middle class schools, the academic track is likely to be predominant. Principal expectations in low socioeconomic schools have been found to reflect those of teachers;[34] when schools were located in low socioeconomic areas, principals were far more likely to predict that their students would move from school directly into work rather than that they would attend either a community or four-year college. When principals and teachers working in schools in low socioeconomic areas do not believe that their students are likely to move into tertiary education, their interactions with and behaviors towards those students are likely to be reflective of their beliefs, and to limit students' chances. When students from low socioeconomic communities are moved to higher tracks, and even to honors classes, they have been shown to be able to achieve at the expected high levels.[35] They just need to be given the opportunity to achieve at high levels and the necessary support to do so.

In some European countries, tracking takes on an even more pernicious role because students are not only tracked into different schools but the different tracks offer very different curricula. As might be predicted, some teachers are better at determining an appropriate track for their students than others,[19] and among the most inaccurate teachers, there can be a mean of a whole track difference. The track to which students are assigned plays a large role in students' futures. In the Netherlands,[19] for example, there are seven different tracks from the lowest which means that when students graduate from high school they will move into some form of practical training, and most likely an unskilled occupation, compared with students at the other end who are assigned a pre-university education and will most likely move into the equivalent of a four-year college when they leave school. The decision about which tracks students will move into is made when students are only 11 years old. Similarly to the United States, students who come from low socioeconomic backgrounds appear to be disadvantaged in terms of track recommendations. In other words, students from less affluent backgrounds are more likely to be assigned to a lower track than what their achievement indicates they should be, and those from wealthier families are given higher track recommendations than they should have. However, some teachers have been found to exaggerate the differences between students from different socioeconomic backgrounds recommending quite different tracks for students achieving at similar levels whereas other teachers tend to be more equitable in their ratings. Also, where classes are high achieving and have only small numbers of students from poorer backgrounds, students are likely to benefit from higher track recommendations than they deserve. Given that the tracks relate closely to the future occupations of the students, inaccurate recommendations by teachers can have serious future consequences for students.

In other countries, for example the United States,[36] Australia,[37] and New Zealand,[38] although students might all attend regular schools, the curriculum offered to different tracks within schools and to students across schools can vary such that the curriculum becomes stratified. This is achieved in several ways. First, students are now offered a far more wide-ranging choice of curriculum than they were many years ago. Many of the subjects that have been added to the curriculum are technical or vocational subjects. If students take these subjects, they may be able to move into employment when they leave high school, but most of these subjects do not lead to college. Second, some curriculum areas have become stratified within them and students may not realize the consequences of taking, for example, general science rather than chemistry or physics. Again, where passes in chemistry or physics at high school may lead to places in courses at college, completing general science may not offer those advantages. Third, in both Australia and New Zealand, students can select subjects whereby they are examined only internally, only externally or a combination of both. However, only those that are wholly examined externally or both internally and externally lead to college. Students, particularly those from low socioeconomic backgrounds where they do not have parental role models who understand how to negotiate the secondary school system, are at an especial disadvantage. Often students will be guided by teachers with low expectations into selecting subjects that do not provide a college pathway or they will be encouraged to pursue subjects that rely mostly on internal assessments.

Teachers can also have far-reaching effects on the outcomes of students from low socioeconomic backgrounds. Sorhagen[39] showed that when teachers underestimated student achievement when they were in first grade, students scored lower on standardized tests when they were 15 years of age. Conversely, when students were overestimated in Grade 1, their scores were higher at 15 years. This finding occurred even when student demographics and previous achievement were accounted for. Further, when teachers had high expectations for students in Grade 1, all students benefitted at age 15 regardless of socioeconomic status. On the other hand, when the language and mathematics skills of students from low socioeconomic backgrounds were underestimated in Grade 1, the self-fulfilling prophecy effects were much stronger than they were for other students; there was a far more deleterious effect on their achievement compared with other students. Hence, students from poorer socioeconomic backgrounds may be more vulnerable to teachers' expectations. Given that students from low socioeconomic backgrounds come from disadvantaged homes, it is important that they are given more opportunities to learn in order to close the gaps; unfortunately, they are often given fewer opportunities – and this reduction in opportunities can have marked consequences on their future employment prospects.

GENDER

A further student characteristic that has been explored in relation to teacher expectations is gender. As is well known, males are more likely to take STEM subjects at college whereas females are more likely to follow a Humanities or Social Science curriculum. This is a choice that clearly leads to different careers. The idea that is explored in this section is whether these choices are influenced by teacher expectations.

Mathematics. Mathematics has traditionally been considered a male domain. Overall, males have tended to take more advanced mathematics courses at high school than females and, on entering college, males are more likely to take mathematics than females. These differences are thought to arise, in part, from teachers' expectations. Teachers have been shown to credit boys with having more natural ability in mathematics whereas when girls have done well in mathematics, this has been attributed to effort.[40] It seems that teachers tend to overrate boys in mathematics and to have higher expectations for them.[41] They perceive boys more positively and therefore interact with them in a more supportive fashion. In turn, the interactions of teachers, may result in girls losing confidence in their ability in mathematics, they may become increasingly aware of the stereotypes surrounding the idea that boys are better at mathematics, may come to perceive mathematics as being too difficult for girls, and may be unsure of how useful mathematics may be for their future careers. However, in classes where teachers expect girls to do just as well as boys in mathematics, the gap between the achievement of boys and girls is much less by the end of the year than at the beginning of the year.[41] Despite this finding, the evidence for whether or not boys achieve in mathematics at higher levels than girls is equivocal with some studies showing that they do achieve at higher levels[42] and others showing that girls' achievement is higher,[43] particularly in the latter years of compulsory schooling.

Science. Similarly to mathematics, science has stereotypically been seen as a male domain, and also, as with mathematics, any differences in achievement between boys and girls may be due to the differential interactions of teachers with boys versus girls. Teachers are more likely to ask low level questions of girls than boys and, conversely, they ask boys more high level questions than girls.[44] Furthermore, overall, teachers interact more frequently with boys than girls in science. The less frequent interactions of girls with their teachers may portray to girls that they are not good at science because, as described earlier in this book, teachers tend to interact less often with those for whom they have low expectations. Teachers have also been shown to have different beliefs about the capability of boys and girls in science, believing that boys are more able than girls.[45] Beliefs such as this become reflected in teacher expectations and, therefore, in the opportunities to learn that are provided by teachers. Lower expectations for girls in science can lead to them being given lower level tasks and assuming more passive roles. For example, boys are much more likely to lead the use of scientific equipment and experiments while girls look on.[45] Further, when girls do achieve highly in science, there is often pressure from other peers, in particular, for girls to conform to the gender stereotypes. So, whereas boys may be lauded for achieving well in science, girls can be subjected to name-calling such as "nerd" or "geek."[46] Even girls who are considered gifted face a similar dilemma; whereas teachers expect them to achieve at high levels and to be academically focused in all curriculum areas, peers consider that gifted girls need to fit in socially with their peer group and that high levels of academic achievement are not so important.[47] Nevertheless, as with mathematics, when teachers have high expectations for girls in science and girls are actively encouraged to pursue their interests, they are much more likely to be successful, to choose more advanced science courses in secondary school, and to pursue a science career in the future.[48]

At the further end of the academic spectrum, even those with doctorates tend to believe that some fields require natural ability rather than effort in order to be successful. Perhaps unsurprisingly these fields are mostly STEM-based: Statistics, biochemistry, chemistry, astronomy, mathematics, engineering, computer science, and physics. Females are represented in these fields in significantly fewer numbers than males. Moreover, the more that any field perceives that innate ability is important for success, the more those working in those fields seem to consider women to be unsuitable for the high levels of scholarly work required and report that they are less welcoming to women.[49]

Literacy. As opposed to mathematics and the sciences, in the area of literacy, girls are generally deemed to be more capable. Teachers tend to expect more of girls in this area and yet, similarly to science and mathematics where more may be expected of boys, in reading, for example, when teachers expect boys to do just as well as girls, by the end of one year, they do, even if they began at lower levels, and, conversely, when teachers expect girls to do better than boys by the end of the year, they do.[50] Similar results have been found in writing. When teachers are given a selection of written language samples to grade but they have no indication of gender, if they believe that the piece of writing has been completed by a girl, they are likely to rate it more favorably than if they think it was written by a boy. Teachers will also credit the same piece of writing with more sophistication in terms of style and content when they believe that a girl wrote it rather than a boy.[51] Even in oral language, when Grades 2 and 3 students were recorded responding to a range of teacher questions and teachers were not told the gender of the child, if they believed that the response was from a girl, they were likely to evaluate it more positively than if they thought it was from a boy. Further, both male and female teachers appear to favor girls when evaluating their literacy skills.[52]

Student behavior. The discussion above has shown that teacher expectations can vary in relation to males and females depending on the curriculum area, and this differentiation can occur from Kindergarten right through to doctoral level. Another area in which teacher expectations have been found to vary by gender is in what teachers expect or consider acceptable in terms of student behavior. Overall, girls are perceived to display more acceptable classroom behavior. Teachers seem to believe that girls behave more favorably in terms of their social interactions, work habits, and attitudes to school.[53] However, when students display what is considered sex-inappropriate behavior, then teachers are more likely to rate such students as demonstrating disturbing behavior and they are likely to have lower expectations of them.[54]

In the United Kingdom, when teachers were interviewed about student attitudes,[55] they reported that boys were untidy and disordered, that they often failed to submit assignments, that work that was submitted was often of a lower than acceptable standard, and that the work was poorly presented. Teachers also reported that boys lacked concentration, motivation, and organization. Teachers believed that these poor attitudes of boys led them to disengage from schoolwork and withdraw their involvement such that, ultimately, they were underachieving compared to girls. The student perspective was different, however. Many boys and a large number of girls believed that girls were more actively encouraged and supported by teachers, and teachers sought to engage them in lessons through questions and many positive interactions. Boys also perceived that teachers had both higher expectations and aspirations for girls; boys felt less valued and that explained their disengagement and reduced effort.

It can be seen that issues of gender in relation to teacher expectations are complex and multi-faceted. It seems that in some curriculum areas girls are overestimated whereas in others the positive expectations apply to boys. Much of this differentiation appears to be related to stereotyping and applies not just to beliefs about gendered subject areas but also in relation to behaviors that are expected or perceived to be displayed by boys compared to girls. As was pointed out earlier in this book, teacher expectations may result in differential teacher interactions with students. These interactions inform students of how well they are expected to do in terms of achievement and behavior. Teachers' expectations and interactions can affect student self-belief and, in turn, may result in the student conforming to their teachers' expectations.

SPECIAL NEEDS STUDENTS

The student characteristics of ethnicity, social class, and gender have probably garnered most attention in relation to teacher expectations. However, the labelling of students as having special needs of some form can also lead to teachers lowering their expectations. Labeling of students will be explored in this section.

Within many education systems, students need to be categorized and labeled as having special needs in order to receive resources to support the students' learning. Without the label, no funding or resources are forthcoming. However, it may be that a cost of resources designed to benefit students is that teachers lower expectations for such students. The language used to describe students needing additional support of one form or another focuses on what students cannot do rather than on what they can. It is a language of disability rather than ability and such language may influence teachers' expectations leading to them lowering expectations and dumbing down the curriculum for those so labelled. If such students are to be successful then there needs to be an expectation that all students can learn and that they will be able to overcome any current discrepancies in their achievement and go on to become successful learners.[56] There is evidence[35,57] that students labelled as low achieving, disabled or at-risk can achieve at high levels given teacher support that ensures such students reach their goals. This requires commitment from teachers and high levels of effort from students. However, the expectation literature is replete with studies showing that labeling appears to lower teachers' expectations and alter the types of learning opportunities provided for students. It is the purpose of this next section in this chapter to discuss how labeling can affect teacher expectations.

Many of the studies that have been completed in this area are experimental. That is, teachers are presented with a scenario and records related to a hypothetical student. In one of these scenarios, the student will have no label. In others of the exact same scenario, students will be given one or more labels (for example, learning, behavioral or emotional difficulties) and teachers then judge how well they perceive that the student will achieve in the next and perhaps subsequent years. Almost always, the findings are that teachers have lower expectations for those with a label compared to those with no label. Nevertheless, it is my belief that in such experimental studies, the teachers do not know the student(s) described; it is not possible to extrapolate the findings to actual classrooms where teachers are interacting on a daily basis with their students and know them well. Further, the participants who are responding to the scenarios are often pre-service teachers who may not have much experience with special needs students. When they do, they may change their expectations.[58] For these reasons, although I do present some findings related to experimental studies, I have privileged those conducted in classrooms with teachers and their actual students (what are called naturalistic studies).

Multiple or encompassing labels. When teachers are asked about their expectations for students with different labels, for example, having a physical disability, a learning disability, or behavioral or emotional difficulties, students with no label seem to be rated more highly than any other group. However, there is no consistency reported in the degree to which particular labels influence expectations. What we do know is that labels influence expectations. This is because expectations lead to a change in teachers' practices and these practices result in student learning opportunities being constrained when they are labeled. For example, among four teachers,[59] one teacher limited the exposure that her students with reading difficulties were given to literacy materials because she did not believe that students would benefit. The others believed that students were capable of learning and would be able to use their developing literacy skills within the broader community, to extend their communications with others and to build relationships. When teachers believed that students could learn and that having literacy skills would benefit their lives in a number of ways, they challenged students and supported their learning. Teachers who believed they could make a difference to student learning and foresaw that student literacy outcomes would be positive, had higher levels of teaching efficacy. They believed in their own skills to support and develop student learning.

Even when student achievement is controlled, those with a history of special education are disadvantaged. This means that even when student achievement is the same but one student has an Individualized Education Program (IEP) whereas another does not, the student without an IEP can be up to five times more likely to be recommended for placement in Algebra at Grade 8 than a student with an IEP.[60] Being enrolled in algebra at Grade 8 often leads to students being able to attend a four-year college. Hence, teacher recommendations can influence student life chances. However, it appears that once students are labeled, teachers tend to underestimate their abilities.

It seems, therefore, that the beliefs of teachers (reflecting their expectations) can have profound consequences for students. However, those consequences do not just relate to the learning and other experiences provided for students with disabilities. Most teachers, and educators generally, would likely express ideas that students with disabilities should be supported and nurtured while they are at school. Unfortunately, that does not always seem to be the case. At times, there have been reports of special needs students being subjected to microaggressions and bullying by teachers and sometimes by teacher aides.[61] Observers have documented instances of students being subjected to sarcasm and tone of voice that clearly communicates low expectations, to insults, belittlement, and name-calling. Special needs students have been told that they are wasting their time being at school and that they will never go to college. Teachers may express surprise when the students do well on a test or assignment. All these interactions clearly communicate teachers' expectations of special needs students. Hence, there may be emotional and psychological consequences for special needs students in school. If they are led to believe that they cannot achieve, it is possible that such information leads to a lowering of self-esteem and sense of competence, and of special needs students becoming de-motivated and, in turn, to declining success. School should be a safe place for all students and that instances of poor behavior by professionals towards vulnerable students have been documented on more than one occasion is distressing. If special needs students are to be successful within the educational environment, they need teachers who believe in them and support their learning.

Learning disabled and educable mentally retarded students. Similarly to what was described above, teachers tend to rate learning disabled and educable mentally retarded students lower than students who are not labelled but who have the same achievement levels. This has been found in both experimental and naturalistic studies in contexts as different as the United States, the United Kingdom, Australia, Finland, and Greece. Regular classroom teachers, special education teachers and parents all tend to underrate learning disabled students.[62,63] In a comparison of the expectations of special versus general education teachers for educable mentally retarded students and students in general classrooms, both groups of students had previously been tested and found to have comparable mental ages and performances on a standardized mathematics test. Special education teachers underestimated their Grade 1 educable mentally retarded students whereas general education teachers overestimated their regular students. Similarly, for Grade 3 learning disabled and normally achieving students with similar IQ scores, ages and socioeconomic background, the expectations of mothers and teachers were compared. Both mothers and teachers had much lower expectations for the learning disabled students and predicted bleaker futures for them, despite the evidence that both groups were achieving at similar levels.

As I have reiterated several times in this book, the concern is not so much that expectations are lower for one group than another (when they should not be) but that lowered expectations often result in reduced opportunities to learn. It is the practices that result from the expectations that is of concern. For example, in inclusive classrooms, teachers mostly focused on the socialization skills of students defined as having severe disabilities. They believed that the academic performance of such students was of little relevance.[64] Hence, even though students were defined as having severe disabilities, teachers were limiting their chances to gain academically because they did not consider them capable. On the other hand, the focus for students with mild disabilities was on the development of classroom and behavior skills, academic performance, and in developing the students' self-confidence.

Once students have been labelled as learning disabled, teachers seem to generalize from one supposed deficit to others. For example, they may consider students labeled as learning disabled to have poorer memories than regular students and to lack memory strategies[65] or they may perceive that learning disabled students have poor social relationships with their peers.[66] Further, in explaining a lack of academic progress among learning disabled students, teachers are likely to attribute this to deficiencies within the child or within their families rather than in the ways in which they are delivering or structuring learning opportunities for the student. It is possible that if teachers took more responsibility for the learning of students labeled disabled and focused on how teaching practices might be changed, the lack of student progress may be ameliorated.[67]

Perhaps not surprisingly, and possibly as an outcome of interactions with teachers and parents, learning disabled students are more likely to have poor self-concepts and to believe that when they are successful in school that it is because of sheer luck or because of other people. They are also likely to believe that they cannot overcome their failures. Sadly, these beliefs become established by the age of nine years and tend to become more negative over time.[68] It is important that the self-beliefs of learning disabled students are strengthened if they are to maintain any form of motivation over time. Teachers and parents have a key role to play in focusing and building on the strengths of learning disabled students rather than on their difficulties. Beliefs that all students can learn are likely to lead to instructional practices that show that learning is amenable to high expectations and positive support.

In an intervention study, Moscardini[69] was able to show that prior to professional development, teachers lacked knowledge about the developmental trajectory of students' mathematical learning and about the best pedagogy for improving student learning. Many held deficit beliefs about, and low expectations for, their learning disabled students. Following professional development, teachers reported that the deeper understanding that they had gained about students' mathematical thinking and development, had provided them with a much firmer base on which to plan for student learning. They changed their views of the learning capabilities of learning disabled students and became much more adept at understanding student errors and misconceptions and how to address these. Studies such as these show that teachers are willing to change their expectations and alter practice in order to facilitate the learning of disabled students. There appears to be a need for professional development that can assist teachers to work more effectively with learning disabled students.

Hearing impaired students. As with the broader categories of learning disabilities, specific impairments have also been investigated. One of those is hearing. Teacher expectations for hearing impaired students have mostly been found to be lower than those for their hearing peers and this may be because of stereotypes that although hearing impaired students can successfully learn to compute, they cannot learn to read or write at similar levels to their hearing peers.[70] Just the sight of a hearing aid can be enough to trigger low teacher expectations.[71]

However, intervention programs[72,73] designed to teach teachers effective ways of instructing their hearing impaired students have been effective in increasing the learning of hearing impaired students and, consequently, raising teachers' expectations that their hearing impaired students will improve, and showing teachers how to provide challenging lessons for their hearing impaired students. Hence, one factor that may contribute to lower teacher expectations may simply relate to training. Once teachers are equipped with strategies to increase the learning of hearing impaired students and can see students improving, their expectations are raised.

An exemplary teacher of hearing impaired students showed that her classroom was premised on high expectation principles.[74] Her high expectations were largely portrayed through the warm, positive class climate that she created for students. She emphasized that students were expected to achieve at the curriculum levels of their peers. To this end, students were given challenging learning experiences and were often asked to explain responses to questions in order to encourage them to think more deeply. The teacher expected the hearing impaired students to show effort, to think for themselves, and to learn from their errors. She held a belief that all her hearing impaired students could learn. Students reported that the teacher respected them, that her attitudes towards them were positive, and that she was helpful. Interestingly, the teacher was hearing impaired herself so this may have led to the uncompromising belief that all her students could succeed. She expected that they would do well – and they were.

Dyslexic students. Students with dyslexia often have difficulty with spelling and writing but are strong in areas such as problem solving, lateral thinking, and high level thinking. When teachers completed a test measuring implicit attitudes towards dyslexia,[75] the results predicted both teachers marking of a student written task and student results on a spelling test for students who were dyslexic. Explicit expectations predicted student outcomes for all students, that is, there were no differences between the degree to which explicit expectations affected dyslexic and non-dyslexic students. It may be that implicit attitudes were more predictive of outcomes for dyslexic students because teachers would realize that presenting a negative attitude about dyslexic students would be socially undesirable. Instead, they showed very positive explicit expectations. Because it is more difficult to conceal implicit attitudes, it may be that these are more reflective of actual attitudes.

Not all teachers, however, held the same degree of negative bias towards students with dyslexia, but teachers who held more negative attitudes gave their dyslexic students lower ratings for their written language and also their students scored lower on a standardized spelling test.[75] While the mediating mechanisms of teacher implicit attitudes are not currently known, it is likely that they are similar to those for explicit expectations. For example, teachers may put in less effort to helping dyslexic students, they may interact with them differently both in terms of quality and quantity, they may provide them with reduced opportunities to respond and provide less useful feedback. Interestingly, implicit attitudes are most often portrayed via nonverbal interactions whereas explicit expectations are more often portrayed verbally. Therefore, it may also be that teachers show less warmth and emotional support towards students with dyslexia. Hence, one way (mentioned earlier) that teachers could check their own interactions is by videotaping lessons (as with ethnic or other biases) and carefully reflecting on how they might be conveying messages to students.

Student behavior. Although we know quite a lot about how labels can influence teachers' expectations, less is known about these same ideas when applied to students with behavioral and emotional difficulties. What is known is possibly predictable. Teacher expectations seem to be lowered when teachers perceive the same described behaviors as pertaining to either behaviorally or emotionally maladjusted students as compared with a student without a label. Furthermore, teachers often have lower academic expectations for students described as displaying externalizing behaviors even though such behaviors are not necessarily related to academics.

Studies in the United States, show that boys are 3.5 times more likely than girls to be receiving specialist services for emotional and/or behavioral difficulties (EBD),[76] and this rate of referral is higher than for any other type of disability. Further, students in poverty are twice as likely to be identified as having EBD as students from middle class homes. In Canada, the findings are similar.[76] Of students identified in the EBD group in Canada, 75 percent were boys (80 percent in the US), and a greater proportion were from poorer families. Generally, students appear to be working with special education services because of externalizing (rather than internalizing) behaviors such as aggression, hyperactivity, and disruption. Teachers tend to rate such students lower on social skills, and the students themselves report having difficulties with friendships and poorer social experiences. EBD students report that teachers treat them fairly. However, students referred to special education services for behavioral difficulties may also be referred for academic performance, even though they may not be having academic problems.[77] Hence, behavior and academic competence may become confounded in teachers' minds.

ADHD and autism. Attention deficit hyperactivity disorder and autism are two particular behavioral patterns that have received a lot of attention both in the media and in terms of school referrals but to date there are only a handful of studies that have investigated teacher attitudes to students with ADHD.[78–80] Even fewer have examined beliefs about students with autism.[78] When presented with identical descriptions of student behavior but where students are labelled ADHD, ADHD but on medication, or no label, teachers rated the labelled students more harshly than students who were not labeled and the ADHD students more negatively than those with ADHD but on medication, even though the only change to the descriptions of students was the labels.[78,80] Teachers also rated students with ADHD and those on medication less favorably for their personality, IQ, and behavior than those who were not labeled. Moreover, those labeled ADHD were rated more harshly in terms of both their behavior and their personality compared with those described as ADHD but on medication. Further, there also appears to be a gender bias with boys being rated more negatively than girls for the same descriptions.[78] There may be a cultural element, too, because in Greece where hyperactivity is accepted, teachers rate students with impulsivity and inattentiveness as impaired in academic and social functioning but these negative attitudes do not present when students are described as hyperactive.[79] Teachers report a level of tension when confronted with ADHD-related classroom behaviors.[81] As with the labeling of other students, when teachers have negative expectations of students with ADHD compared to their peers, this is likely to translate into teacher behaviors that increase the probability that students will behave in accordance with teachers' expectations.

In terms of students with autism and teacher expectations, little is known. Teacher perceptions of the importance of various outcomes for students with autism versus whether or not teachers expected these outcomes would be achieved have been explored.[82] Teachers believed that autistic students needed a network of friends, to be accepted, to be kept physically safe, to become socially responsible, to take care of their parents when they were elderly, to participate in extracurricular activities, to learn to live independently, to find a job, to be happy and satisfied in their lives, to have a stable financial future, to have the highest education possible, and to make use of community services. However, for all of these outcomes, teachers held much lower expectations that autistic students would achieve any of them. Hence, they believed a number of life opportunities were important for autistic students but believed that the likelihood of them actually achieving those outcomes was low.

This fairly lengthy section related to students with special needs has shown that even when other students' academic performance and behaviors are similar or exactly the same, teachers still tend to rate them lower than students who are not labeled. This is concerning given the change in teacher behaviors that can result from low expectations, the reduced opportunities for learning that can follow, and the less positive interactions that special needs students may then be subjected to. When students already have difficulties to overcome that are associated with their various disabilities to have to also overcome low teacher expectations is disappointing. It is important that students are assessed objectively and fairly. Becoming aware of the potential biasing effects of labeling may help teachers to reflect more carefully when working with and evaluating their students diagnosed with special needs.

Student Characteristics

This part of the chapter has described the four student characteristics most frequently researched and most often found to influence teacher expectations: Ethnicity, social class, gender, and special needs. The remainder of the chapter will focus on other characteristics of students that have been less frequently investigated: Gifted students, family circumstances, names, English second language, names, attractiveness, and personality.

GIFTED

I realize that gifted students are also often classified as special needs students. However, because they are regularly viewed quite differently to students for whom learning may be a struggle, and because the findings pertaining to gifted students are somewhat different to those for other special needs students, I have chosen to highlight the place of gifted students and teacher expectations in a separate section in this chapter.

There is not a lot known about relations between teacher expectations and gifted students. Concerns include gifted students who underachieve and lower teacher expectations for gifted students from minority groups. When gifted African American students described their experiences with teachers they considered effective and ineffective, their evaluations were illuminating.[83] They described ineffective teachers as having low expectations of them, developing an intimidating and unfriendly classroom environment, allowing peers to insult and humiliate them, showing surprise when African American students were considered gifted, and not providing a multi-cultural curriculum. On the other hand, effective teachers had high expectations of all students, promoted cooperative learning, accommodated student learning preferences, praised and encouraged their students, had a student-centered classroom, paid attention to developing positive relationships in the classroom, incorporated a multicultural curriculum into their teaching, involved students' families in the classroom, and encouraged the students to connect with mentors and role models.

Minority groups are under-represented in gifted programs. Other than low expectations, the (in)ability of teachers to accurately identify gifted students may be one reason for why minority groups are underrepresented. When gifted readers were identified by researchers from their reading scores on a standardized test,[84] over 20 percent of students were misclassified by teachers with expectations for gifted students ranging from rating them as very much below average to only slightly above average. More girls than boys were underestimated and, in particular, more minority group girls were underestimated. Further, teachers did not adjust their expectations upwards later in the year despite having standardized test data available. Hence, within the area of teacher expectations and gifted students, it would seem that there is an urgent need for teacher training that may help teachers to become more accurate in their assessments of their gifted students and thereby provide more appropriately for their needs. It is possible that the lack of accuracy in teacher expectations and resulting practices are contributing to the underachievement of some gifted learners.

PERSONAL AND FAMILY CIRCUMSTANCES

Various personal and family circumstances (other than socioeconomic status) have been investigated as potentially detrimentally impacting teacher expectations. These include students who have been sexually abused, in foster care, whose parents (particularly mothers) are incarcerated, who have a baby, whose parents are divorced, whose mothers work, who have been exposed to drugs, who are in prison themselves, or who are obese. In all of these situations, the expectations mostly follow predictable patterns and teachers anticipate that students in these circumstances are likely to have more bleak futures than other students.

Therefore, rather than expound confirming evidence, I will concentrate on presenting some contrary findings.

Teachers do not necessarily have lower expectations for sexually abused students, particularly female teachers. Although they believe that sexually abused students may be stressed and in need of emotional support, they do not always think that such students are likely to do any worse academically than other students.[85]

Similarly, although expectations do tend to be low for long-term foster care students, this is mostly because achievement is low; expectations are related to achievement. However, because foster care students are often achieving at below average levels, this implies that teachers need to provide greater challenge and support if the students are to increase their rate of progress in order to meet at least average standards.[86]

Students in even the most debilitating of circumstances can be successful academically with a supportive teacher who is prepared to make extra efforts for her students. Students who are incarcerated represent a group at the lowest levels of society. However, despite their own lack of confidence and self-deprecation, coupled with on-going jibes, humiliation, and mockery from prison staff and administrators, one teacher showed what could be done when she had faith in her students. She expected the very best of all her students studying a college-level course. She encouraged their thinking, provided ample feedback on any work, taught curriculum of interest to the students, and provided them with clear learning goals. As a result, many were able to pass the course.[87]

ENGLISH SECOND LANGUAGE AND USE OF NON-STANDARD ENGLISH

Generally teachers seem to have lower expectations for ESL students than for English native speakers. It was argued recently[88] that this led to teachers reducing the curriculum opportunities for ESL students, providing low-level tasks, and accepting low engagement from these students. In other words, they were not offered the advantages of high level cognitive and linguistic challenges that were likely to lead to their success in school. Nevertheless, there are indications that for ESL students moving into the university environment, that their teachers overestimate their English grammatical knowledge.[89] It is thought that this may lead to teachers using grammatical terminology with which learners may not be familiar resulting in confusion for students and inadequate time being spent on teaching ESL students' grammatical ideas that teachers assume they know. Further, in a recent classroom study,[90] teachers were found to overestimate all their students (non-immigrant, bilingual immigrant, non-immigrant), but particularly their bilingual immigrant students, even when taking achievement into account. German teachers were likely to overestimate how well their bilingual students were likely to do on mathematical problems that were linguistically high. It was posited that teachers are not always aware of the linguistic demands of some mathematics problems and may not understand the language difficulties that bilingual students encounter. Together, these examples of too low and too high expectations for students stress the need for teachers to develop an understanding of the individual needs of their students and to use those in implementing tasks that will challenge students' learning but also be achievable.

Students who speak a non-standard form of English may be subjected to low teacher expectations. At times they are diagnosed as having a learning disability and are referred to special education.[91] In the same way that effective teachers have learned to use the first language of ESL students as a resource, it is important that teachers use the dialect of particular students as a resource from which to increase their language use rather than insisting that the student use standard English. Dialects are often associated with particular cultural traditions and group affiliations so it is important that teachers portray respect for the student's home language and encourage the use of the dialect alongside standard English.[91] An awareness of the biasing effect of a dialect is the first step in teachers evaluating students' language fairly.

STUDENT NAMES

It would seem obvious that a student's name should not affect teachers' expectations. Nevertheless, there is some suggestion that names may be associated with increasing or lowering teachers' expectations. It seems that teachers may stereotype students based on names. For example, certain first names are associated with students coming from low socioeconomic groups and from certain ethnic groups, and this can lead to a lowering of expectations. Students with unusual names are less likely to be recommended for gifted programs, even when their scores are the same as those of other students.[92] Further, ethnic sounding names can lead teachers to expect less of students' behavioral achievement.[93]

ATTRACTIVENESS

In a synthesis of early studies from the 1970s and early 1980s,[94] physically attractive students were evaluated more positively on a number of aspects such as intelligence, future academic achievement, grades, and a range of social skills. This applied whether students were in elementary, high school, or college. However, the studies were all experimental. When teachers rated their own six-year-olds,[95] those they assessed as being more attractive, were also rated as better behaved, having higher intelligence, being more interested in school, likely to be successful in life, more popular, and having parents who were more interested in their education, when compared with students the teachers rated as less attractive. Similarly, when teachers evaluated their 11–12-year-old students on attractiveness and then made judgments about their social skills, popularity among peers, how smart and how confident they were, and the quality of the leadership skills, attractive students were rated more highly than students teachers considered less attractive.[96] Further, when the students were tracked, it was found that the teachers' estimate of how smart students were at 11–12 years was a very good predictor of their academic success at 18 years. Students considered attractive by teachers at 11–12 had achieved at higher levels at 18 years than their unattractive peers. Of course, it is unlikely that attractiveness caused the academic success but it may be that along the way, attractive students were given more learning opportunities by their teachers and encouraged more such that eventually they achieved more. At this stage, we simply do not know.

PERSONALITY AND SELF-BELIEF FACTORS

From a teacher perspective, it may seem reasonable to think that students with good social skills are easy to like and that, therefore, teachers may have higher expectations for such students. But this is not an area that has received much attention. Teacher expectations do seem to relate to student self-concept but self-concept also relates to student achievement so expectations may be high for students with positive self-concept simply because achievement is high.[97] In other words, it is completely probable that it is achievement driving expectations rather than student self-concept.

Nevertheless, there may be a relationship between students with high levels of social skills (aspects such as sensitivity to others, willingness to help others and to collaborate, positive leadership qualities, security, and inner strength) and teacher expectations. Teachers tend to have higher expectations for students who possess high levels of social skills such as those mentioned above.[98] However, a cautionary note is warranted because students who are more sensitive, collaborative, and show empathy towards others, also have higher academic achievement – and teacher expectations relate to achievement as well as social skills. Teachers tend to have lower expectations for those who show antisocial behaviors such as being apathetic, withdrawn, or dominant and aggressive, but these students also score lower on achievement than the prosocial group.[98]

CONCLUSION

Investigating students' characteristics as a precursor to teachers' expectations has been the largest area of endeavor within the field. Teacher expectations as a field was founded on the premise that some students were gaining from the education system whereas others were losing. Education came to be viewed as a means of maintaining the social structure; it was not equitable. Therefore, investigations in the teacher expectation field are focused on issues of equity. The idea that some students benefit from the education system whereas others do not is pernicious. This is one reason why the idea that some students are advantaged because of a particular characteristic whereas others may be disadvantaged by the same characteristic that they have no control over, has been investigated over and over. Teachers must be seen as equity-promoting. They are the most important professionals in our society. Teachers have the power to shape the next generation, to transform lives, and to alter life chances; no other profession does that. Teachers have an enormous responsibility in terms of providing equitable opportunities for all students.

Teaching is complex and teachers are human beings. It is likely that they will favor some students over others at least some time in their career. What is important is that, as far as possible, students are not aware of any bias; students should never be penalized because of some arbitrary characteristic; they should not be disadvantaged because they are a particular ethnicity, gender, social class, and so on.

One factor to be remembered is that, above, the point was made that whatever student characteristic was being reported, not all teachers would be swayed; not all teachers buy into stereotypes and adopt them. And that is the major focus of the next chapter – the idea that teachers are individuals, too, and that they will have different beliefs, different values, different expectations. Some teachers will disadvantage students; others will positively transform the life possibilities of their students. The beliefs of individual teachers and how their pedagogy is enacted will moderate expectation effects and many, many teachers have amazing positive effects on all their learners.

REFERENCES

1. Tenenbaum HR, Ruck MD. Are teachers' expectations different for racial minority than for European American students? A meta-analysis. *Journal of Educational Psychology.* 2007;99:253–273.
2. de Boer H, Bosker RJ, Van der Werf M. Sustainability of teacher expectation bias effects on long-term student performance. *Journal of Educational Psychology.* 2010;102:168–179.
3. Rubie-Davies CM, Hattie J, Hamilton R. Expecting the best for New Zealand students: Teacher expectations and academic outcomes. *British Journal of Educational Psychology.* 2006;76:429–444.
4. McKown C, Weinstein RS. Teacher expectations, classroom context and the achievement gap. *Journal of School Psychology.* 2008;46:235–261.
5. Ali J, McInerney DW, Craven RG, Yeung AS, King RB. Socially oriented motivational goals and academic achievement: Similarities between Native and Anglo Americans. *The Journal of Educational Research.* 2014;107:123–137.
6. Moon SS, Blakey JM, Boyas J, Horton K, Kim YJ. The influence of parental, peer, and school factors on marijuana use among native American adolescents. *Journal of Social Service Research.* 2014;40:147–159.
7. Divoky D. The model minority goes to school. *The Phi Delta Kappan.* 1988;70:219–222.

8. Entwisle DR, Alexander KL. Factors affecting achievement test scores and marks of black and white first graders. *The Elementary School Journal*. 1988;88:449–471.
9. Masten WG, Plata M, Wenglar K, Thedford J. Acculturation and teacher ratings of Hispanic and Anglo-American students. *Roeper Review*. 1999;22:64–65.
10. Rampaul WE, Singh M, Didyk J. The relationship between academic achievement, self-concept, creativity and teacher expectations among Native children in a northern Manitoba school. *Alberta Journal of Educational Research*. 1984;30:213–225.
11. Riley T, Ungerleider C. Self-fulfilling prophecy: How teachers' attributions, expectations, and stereotypes influence the learning opportunities afforded Aboriginal students. *Canadian Journal of Education*. 2012;35:303–333.
12. Babad EY. Expectancy bias in scoring as a function of ability and ethnic labels. *Psychological Reports*. 1980;46:625–626.
13. Crozier G. South Asian parents' aspirations versus teachers' expectations in the United Kingdom. *Theory Into Practice*. 2009;48:290–296.
14. Huss-Keeler RL. Teacher perception of ethnic and linguistic minority parental involvement and its relationships to children's language and literacy learning: A case study. *Teaching and Teacher Education*. 1997;13:171–182.
15. Strand S. The White British-Black Caribbean achievement gap: Tests, tiers and teacher expectations. *British Educational Research Journal*. 2012;38:75–101.
16. Gillborn D, Rollock N, Vincent C, Ball SJ. "You got a pass, so what more do you want?": Race, class and gender intersections in the educational experiences of the black middle class. *Race, Ethnicity and Education*. 2012;15:121–139.
17. Glock S, Krolak-Schwerdt S. Does nationality matter? The impact of stereotypical expectations on student teachers' judgments. *Social Psychology of Education*. 2013;16:111–127.
18. Glock S, Krolak-Schwerdt S, Pit-ten Cate IM. Are school placement recommendations accurate? The effect of students' ethnicity on teachers' judgments and recognition memory. *European Journal of Psychology in Education*. 2015;30:169-188.
19. Timmermans AC, Kuyper H, van der Werf MPC. Accurate, inaccurate or biased teacher expectations: Do Dutch teachers differ in their expectations at the end of primary education? *British Journal of Educational Psychology*. 2015;85:459–478.
20. Dandy J, Durkin K, Barber BL, Houghton S. Academic expectations of Australian students from Aboriginal, Asian and Anglo backgrounds:

Perspectives of teachers, trainee teachers and students. *International Journal of Disability, Development and Education.* 2015;62:60–82.
21. Bishop R, Berryman M. *Culture speaks: Cultural relationships and classroom learning.* Wellington, New Zealand: Huia; 2006.
22. Turner H, Rubie-Davies CM, Webber M. Teacher expectations, ethnicity and the achievement gap. *New Zealand Journal of Educational Studies.* 2015;50:1–15.
23. Rubie-Davies CM. *Becoming a high expectation teacher: Raising the bar.* London: Routledge; 2015.
24. Bishop R, Berryman M. Te Kotahitanga: Culturally responsive professional development for teachers. *Paper presented at the Annual Meeting of the American Educational Research Association.* Denver, Colorado 2010, May.
25. Peterson ER, Rubie-Davies C, Osborne D, Sibley C. Teachers' explicit expectations and implicit prejudiced attitudes to educational achievement: Relations with student achievement and the ethnic achievement gap. *Learning and Instruction.* 2016;42:123–140.
26. Rubie-Davies CM, Peterson ER. Relations between teachers' achievement over- and underestimation, and students' beliefs for Māori and Pākehā students. *Contemporary Educational Psychology.* 2016;47:72–83
27. Rist RC. Student social class and teacher expectations: The self-fulfilling prophecy in ghetto education. *Harvard Educational Review.* 1970;40:411–451.
28. Barclay JR, Stilwell WF, Barclay LK. The influence of paternal occupation on social interaction measures in elementary school children. *Journal of Vocational Behavior.* 1972;2:433–466.
29. Dusek J, Joseph G. The bases of teacher expectancies: A meta-analysis. *Journal of Educational Psychology.* 1983;75:327–346.
30. Plewis I. Inferences about teacher expectations from national assessment at Key Stage One. *British Journal of Educational Psychology.* 1997;67:235–247.
31. Westphal A, Becker M, Vock M, Maaz K, Neumann M, McElvany N. The link between teacher-assigned grades and classroom socioeconomic composition: The role of classroom behavior, motivation, and teacher characteristics. *Contemporary Educational Psychology.* 2016;46:218–227.
32. Barbarin OA, Aikens N. Overcoming the educational disadvantages of poor children: How much do teacher preparation, workload and expectations matter? *American Journal of Orthopsychiatry.* 2015;2015:101–105.
33. Timperley HS. School improvement and teachers' expectations of student achievement. *New Zealand Journal of Educational Studies.* 2003;38:73–88.
34. Lewis T, Cheng S-Y. Tracking, expectations, and the transformation of vocational education. *American Journal of Education.* 2006;113:67–99.

35. Weinstein RS, Soule CR, Collins F, Cone J, Mehlhorn M, Simontacchi K. Expectations and high school change: Teacher-researcher collaboration to prevent school failure. *American Journal of Community Psychology.* 1991;19:333–363.
36. Gamoran A, Nystrand M, Berends M, LePore PC. An organizational analysis of the effects of ability grouping. *American Educational Research Journal.* 1995;32:687–715.
37. Tranter D. Unequal schooling: How the curriculum keeps students from low socio-economic backgrounds out of university. *International Journal of Inclusive Education.* 2012;16:901–916.
38. Hynds A, Averill R, Hiindle R, Meyer LH. School expectations and student aspirations: The influence of schools and teachers on Indigenous secondary students. *Ethnicities.* In press.
39. Sorhagen NS. Early teacher expectations disproportionately affect poor children's high school performance. *Journal of Educational Psychology.* 2013;105:465–477.
40. Fennema E, Peterson PL, Carpenter TP, Lubinski CA. Teachers' attributions and beliefs about girls, boys and mathematics. *Educational Studies in Mathematics.* 1990;21:55–69.
41. Li Q. Teachers' beliefs and gender differences in mathematics: A review. *Educational Research.* 1999;41:63–76.
42. Robinson-Cimpian JP, Lubienski ST, Ganley CM. Teachers' perceptions of students' mathematics proficiency may exacerbate early gender gaps in achievement. *Developmental Psychology.* 2014;50:1262–1281.
43. Ding CS, Song K, Richardson LI. Do mathematical gender differences continue? A longitudinal study of gender difference and excellence in mathematics performance in the US. *Educational Studies* 2006;40:279–295.
44. Barba R, Cardinale L. Are females invisible students? An investigation of teacher-student questioning interactions. *School Science and Mathematics.* 1991;91:306–310.
45. Shepardson DP, Pizzini EL. Gender bias in female elementary teachers' perceptions of the scientific ability of students. *Science Education.* 1992;76:147–153.
46. Wong ED. Students' scientific explanations and the contexts in which they occur. *The Elementary School Journal.* 1996;96:495–509.
47. Bretz D. A comparison of attitudes and expectations of teachers and peers towards rural gifted female adolescents. *Research in the Schools.* 2000;7:31–36.

48. Hatchell H. Girls' entry into higher secondary sciences. *Gender and Education*. 1998;10:375–386.
49. Leslie S-J, Cimpian A, Meyer M, Freeland E. Expectations of brilliance underlie gender distributions across disciplines. *Science*. 2015;347:262–265.
50. Palardy J. What teachers believe – what children achieve. *Elementary School Journal*. 1969;69:370–374.
51. Peterson S. Evaluation and teachers' perceptions of gender in sixth-grade student writing. *Research in the Teaching of English*. 1998;33:181–208.
52. Shepherd MA. Effects of ethnicity and gender on teachers' evaluation of students' spoken responses. *Urban Education*. 2011;46:1011–1028.
53. Bognar CJ. Expectations and student characteristics. *Canadian Journal of Education*. 1983;8:47–56.
54. Schlosser L, Algozzine B. Sex, behavior, and teacher expectancies. *The Journal of Experimental Education*. 1980;48:231–236.
55. Younger M, Warrington M. Differential achievement of girls and boys at GCSE: Some observations from the perspective of one school. *British Journal of Sociology of Education*. 1996;17:299–313.
56. Solity J. Reframing psychological assessment. *Educational and Child Psychology*. 1996;13:94–102.
57. Weinstein RS, Worrell FC, eds. *Achieving college dreams: How a university-charter district partnership created an early college high school*. New York: Oxford University Press; 2016.
58. VanWeelden K, Whipple J. Preservice music teachers' predictions, perceptions and assessment of students with special needs: The need for training in student assessment. *Journal of Music Therapy*. 2007;44:74–84.
59. Ruppar AL, Gaffney JS, Dymond SK. Influences on teachers' decisions about literacy for secondary students with severe disabilities. *Exceptional Children*. 2015;81:209–226.
60. Faulkner VN, Crossland CL, Stiff LV. Predicting eighth-grade algebra placement for students with individualized education programs. *Exceptional Children*. 2013;79:329–345.
61. Davila B. Critical race theory, disability microaggressions and latina/o student experiences in special education. *Race Ethnicity and Education*. 2015;18:443–468.
62. Boersma FJ, Chapman JW. Teachers' and mothers' academic achievement expectations for learning disabled children. *Journal of School Psychology*. 1982;20:216–221.

63. Thurman RL, Richardson LI, Bassler OC. An analysis of teacher rating differences between first-grade and mentally retarded children: Were expectancy biases involved? *Educational Research Quarterly.* 1982;7:7–14.
64. Cameron DL, Cook BG. General education teachers' goals and expectations for their included students with mild and severe disabilities. *Education and Training in Autism and Developmental Disabilities.* 2013;48:18–30.
65. Arabsolghar F, Elkins J. Comparative expectations of teachers and parents with regard to memory skills in children with intellectual disabilities. *Journal of Intellectual & Developmental Disability.* 2000;25:169–179.
66. Martinek TJ, Karper WB. Teachers' expectations for handicapped and non-handicapped children in mainstream physical education classes. *Perceptual and Motor Skills.* 1981;53:327–330.
67. Con Way A. Teachers' explanations for children with learning difficulties: An analysis of written reports. *Early Child Development and Care.* 1989;53:53–61.
68. Bryan TH, Pearl RA. Self-concepts and locus of control of learning disabled children. *Educational Horizons.* 1981;59:91–96.
69. Moscardini L. Primary special school teachers' knowledge and beliefs about supporting learning in numeracy. *Journal of Research in Special Educational Needs.* 2015;15:37–47.
70. Williams CB. Expecting the best: The essential lesson for teachers. *Odyssey: New Directions in Deaf Education.* 2014;15:30–34.
71. Cox LR, Cooper WA, McDade HL. Teachers' perceptions of adolescent girls who wear hearing aids. *Language, Speech, and Hearing Services in Schools.* 1989;20:372–380.
72. Walker L, Munro J, Rickards FW. Teaching inferential reading strategies through pictures. *The Volta Review.* 2000;100:105–120.
73. Wu C-JD, Brown PM. Parents' and teachers' expectations of auditor-verbal therapy. *The Volta Review.* 2004;104:5–20.
74. Smith DH. Giving the spoon back: Higher teacher expectations of achievement for students who are deaf. *The Qualitative Report.* 2008;13:657–694.
75. Hornstra L, Denessen E, Bakker J, van den Bergh L, Voeten M. Teacher attitudes toward dyslexia: Effects on teacher expectations and the academic achievement of students with dyslexia. *Journal of Learning Disabilities.* 2010;43:515–529.
76. Whitley J, Lupart JL, Beran T. The characteristics and experiences of Canadian students receiving special education services for emotional/behavioural difficulties. *Exceptionality Education International.* 2009;19:14–31.

Student Characteristics 107

77. Abidin RR, Robinson LL. Stess, biases or professionalism: What drives teachers' referral judgments of students with challenging behaviors? *Journal of Emotional and Behavioral Disorders*. 2002;10:204–212.
78. Batzle CS, Weyandt LL, Janusis GM, DeVietti TL. Potential impact of ADHD with stimulant medication label on teacher expectations. *Journal of Attention Disorders*. 2010;14:157–166.
79. Kakouros E, Maniadaki K, Papaeliou C. How Greek teachers perceive school functioning of pupils with ADHD. *Emotional and Behavioural Difficulties*. 2004;9:41–53.
80. Stinnett TA, Crawford SA, Gillespie MD, Cruce MK, Langford CA. Factors affecting treatment acceptability for psychostimulant medication versus psychoeducational intervention. *Psychology in the Schools*. 2001;38:585–591.
81. Hepperlen TM, Clay DL, Henly GA, Barke CR. Measuring teacher attitudes and expectations toward students with ADHD: Development of the Test of Knowledge about ADHD (KADD). *Journal of Attention Disorders*. 2002;5:133–142.
82. Ivey JK. Outcomes for students with autism spectrum disorders: What is important and likely according to teachers. *Education and Training in Autism and Developmental Disabilities*. 2007;42:3–13.
83. Harmon D. They won't teach me: The voices of gifted African American inner-city students. *Roeper Review*. 2002;24:68–75.
84. Garrett L, Rubie-Davies C, Alansari M, Peterson ER, Flint A, McDonald L, Watson P. Missing out? The potential consequences of inaccurate teacher expectations on young gifted readers' achievement outcomes. *APEX: The New Zealand Journal of Gifted Education*. 2015;19. Online: http://www.giftedchildren.org.nz/apex/v19no1.php
85. O'Donohue W, O'Hare E. How do teachers react to children labeled as sexually abused? *Child Maltreatment*. 1997;2:46–51.
86. Heath AF, Colton MJ, Aldgate J. Failure to escape: A longitudinal study of foster children's educational attainment. *The British Journal of Social Work*. 1994;24:241–260.
87. Farrell CC. Pygmalion in the prison classroom. *International Journal of Offender Therapy and Comparative Criminology*. 1986;30:151–162.
88. Wedin A. A restricted curriculum for second language learners – a self-fulfilling teacher strategy? *Language and Education*. 2010;24:171–183.
89. Berry R. Teachers' awareness of learners' knowledge: The case of metalinguistic terminology. *Language Awareness*. 1997;6:136–146.

Student Characteristics

90. Hachfeld A, Anders Y, Schroeder S, Stanat P, Kunter M. Does immigration background matter? How teachers' predictions of students' performance relate to student background. *International Journal of Educational Research*. 2010;49:78–91.
91. Cheatham GA, Armstrong J, Santos RM. "Y'all listenin?": Accessing children's dialects in preschool. *Young Exceptional Children*. 2009;12:1–13.
92. Vail K. What's in a Name? Maybe, a Student's Grade! *Education Digest: Essential Readings Condensed for Quick Review*. 2005;71:41–43.
93. Ambady N, Laplante D, Nguyen T, Rosenthal R, Chaumeton N, Levinson W. Surgeons' tone of voice: A clue to malpractice history. *Surgery*. 2002;132:5–9.
94. Ritts V, Patterson ML, Tubbs ME. Expectations, impressions, and judgments of physically attractive students: A review. *Review of Educational Research*. 1992;62:413–426.
95. Dare GJ. The effect of pupil appearance on teacher expectations. *Early Child Development and Care*. 1992;80:97–101.
96. Kenealy P, Frude N, Shaw W. Teacher expectations as predictors of academic success. *Journal of Social Psychology*. 1991;131:305–306.
97. Hay I, Ashman AF, Van Kraayenoord CE. Educational characteristics of students with high or low self-concept. *Psychology in the Schools*. 1998;35:391–400.
98. Jimenez Morales A, Lopez Zafra E. The impact of students' perceived emotional intelligence, social attitudes and teacher expectations on academic performance. *Electronic Journal of Research in Educational Psychology*. 2013;11:75–98.

Four
Teacher Differences in Propensity for Expectation Effects

The crux of this chapter is the individuality of teachers and how that relates to their teaching. It asks questions such as: Do teachers differ in their susceptibility to producing positive or negative expectation effects? If so, is this susceptibility amenable to change? In other words, are expectation effects universal across teachers or do teacher differences play a role in their beliefs and practices toward individual students or classes as a whole? Can the capacity for high expectations for all students be taught?

The vast majority of studies in the field of teacher expectations have focused on the differential expectations that teachers have for their students, that they have for students from particular groups, and the ways in which their expectations are enacted, such that those for whom they have high expectations are treated very differently from those for whom they have low expectations. From this perspective, teachers are considered one group: Do teachers have high expectations for some students and low for others? If so, are there particular students for whom teacher expectations are high or low? When teachers have high expectations for some students and low for others, how are these expectations portrayed in the classroom? Do students detect the differential ways in which students are treated? In answering all of these questions, the focus is firmly on grouping all teachers together, as if they are all the same, and examining differentiation via types of students. A relatively small group of researchers has focused on teacher differences and the idea that teachers are not one group, that there are likely particular beliefs that one group of teachers holds versus another that lead them to teach in different ways – their beliefs and their pedagogical practices likely moderate the expectation effects.

This means that in relation to all the findings presented in the previous three chapters, there will be some teachers who have much larger effects on their students and others whose effects are much weaker. The expectations of some teachers will be positively biased whereas those of other teachers will be negatively biased. Some teachers will assimilate the societal stereotypes into their belief system and treat particular groups of students very differently from others; other teachers will reject the stereotypes and treat students as individuals. Some teachers will teach in ways that students have always been taught, wherever they are based. Other teachers will question current practices and develop their own teaching philosophies. Some teachers will be confident, strong, effective practitioners; others will not. Almost any characteristic of teaching and teachers that can be thought of will see teachers on a continuum because not all teachers are the same. They are individuals such that the teaching in every classroom and the interactions therein will differ.

PROACTIVE, REACTIVE AND OVER-REACTIVE TEACHERS

Brophy and Good[1] conducted extensive observations in classrooms. They noticed and noted that not all teachers created self-fulfilling prophecy effects among their students, and when they did, some created positive effects, others negative. As early as 1974, they proposed that whether or not teachers were susceptible to teacher expectation effects depended very much on the individual teacher. Brophy and Good proposed three types of teachers based on their observations: Proactive, reactive, and over-reactive teachers.

Proactive teachers are those who have firmly developed pedagogical beliefs about what is appropriate for their students and will adapt their teaching style to meet the needs of different students. They will normally have the skill to be able to set realistic goals for their students and will be able to support students to systematically move them towards meeting their expectations that underpin the goals. They will support students when they meet obstacles along the way or become frustrated, adapting their teaching in ways that help students; they take responsibility for their students' learning, rather than blaming the student when tasks are difficult. The expectation effects of proactive teachers are likely to be positive and low achievers are likely to benefit.

Over-reactive teachers are quite different. It is these teachers who are likely to assimilate stereotypes about groups into their belief system and then to treat students as reflective of those stereotypes, rather than treating students as individuals. Over-reactive teachers are the most likely to have negative expectation effects on their students, especially those who are low achievers and those from a stereotyped group. Depending on their teaching skill, high achievers may benefit from being in the classes of over-reactive teachers but if the teacher does not possess a high level of teaching skill, they may also suffer. It is possible that in the classes of over-reactive teachers, the gap between high and low achievers would widen as the academic year progressed.

The majority of teachers would be what were termed reactive teachers. These teachers do not keep trying to make students meet their expectations of them nor do they treat students as representing particular stereotypes. Reactive teachers are likely to adjust their expectations when they see how students are progressing. Student learning gains or lack of progress inform new expectations. These teachers are likely to have the smallest expectation effects on their students. Instead, existing student differences are likely to be maintained; the gap between highs and lows is not likely to increase but nor is it likely to decrease.

Proactive, reactive, and over-reactive teachers were proposed based on extensive classroom observations. However, whether these teachers could actually be identified in classrooms, what the personal characteristics of these teachers might be, and what their pedagogical beliefs were, were never actually tested in classrooms. Nevertheless, the idea that teachers are individuals who are likely to differ in many ways was picked up by other researchers.

BIASED AND UNBIASED TEACHERS

Elisha Babad had worked with Robert Rosenthal on several experimental studies. Many of these types of studies were represented in the previous chapter whereby teachers are presented with a scenario about a student and the only thing that will change in the description will be some form of demographic information at the beginning of the scenario. For example, teachers might be given a piece of written work which they are asked to evaluate. Every teacher will receive the same piece of written language but for some teachers, the written language will be purported to have come from a boy whereas for other teachers it will be purported to come from a girl. Other demographic information might also be manipulated in the same experiment. For example, the writing could be claimed to have been completed by an African American student versus a White student. An extension of this experiment would be that teachers would grade two pieces of work deemed to be equivalent in quality but with the demographic information being manipulated. When teachers graded the work differently depending on the purported author, they would be deemed to be biased.

Elisha Babad conducted a program of work whereby he was able to identify teachers who were biased versus teachers who did not show any bias.[2] In his studies, he used an IQ test called the Draw-a-Person test. He taught teachers how to score student drawings based on the manual for the test. For example, students are scored based on the amount of detail included in the drawing and the accuracy in positioning of body parts. Babad then provided teachers with two drawings to score, one of which was purported to have been drawn by a student from a family whose parents had low skilled occupations and from a minority ethnic group and one from a family whose parents were highly skilled and were from the majority group. Actually the drawing came from the test manual so Babad knew the scores that the drawings should receive. There was a difference of three points between the drawing he had said was from the high status student versus that from the low. Hence, he could calculate the level of bias of each teacher by subtracting their scores for the two drawings from each other. Those for whom the points differed by more than three points could be considered biased.

Around one-sixth of the teachers showed no bias; they scored the drawings in line with the training that they had been given. Approximately half the teachers showed a small degree of bias scoring the high status student a little higher than they deserved. One quarter of teachers were categorized as highly biased; they assigned a much higher score to the high status student than to the low. Finally, a very small group of teachers (3 to 5 percent) were considered to show reverse bias. That is, they scored the low-status student's drawing higher than that of the high status student.

Babad conducted further investigations of highly biased teachers. Interestingly, their characteristics were similar to the over-reactive teachers described earlier. A range of attributes typified biased teachers. They were intolerant of ambiguity, and they held both more extreme political and educational views than unbiased teachers. They also showed what is termed a "halo effect" whereby for low expectation students, for example, biased teachers generalized low achievement to many other negative traits that the student seemingly possessed. Biased teachers also had difficulties processing more complex ideas and information. Interestingly, when biased teachers were asked to describe themselves from an adjective checklist, they portrayed themselves as less biased, more reasonable, logical, and objective than did unbiased teachers.

Observations of biased and unbiased teachers' nonverbal behavior showed that biased teachers were less capable of hiding their true feelings, especially their negative feelings, from their students than were unbiased teachers.[3] This meant that their negativity was portrayed to students through their voice tone and body language. Further, classroom observations showed that unbiased teachers were simply more effective teachers in terms of the ways in which they interacted with students, their general demeanor in the classroom towards students, and their pedagogy. This was in stark contrast to the practices of biased teachers. These observations were confirmed from evaluations by the teachers' supervisors who were not aware of the basis of the researcher's observations.

Biased and unbiased teachers nominated three high expectation and three low expectation students and were told that two of their students were those likely to substantially improve their performance that year.[4] The teachers were then observed and their interactions with the eight selected students meticulously recorded. Student performance on the various tasks set by their teachers were also measured. Expectancy effects were evident in the classes of biased but not unbiased teachers. The biased teachers treated their high and low expectation students very differently and were particularly negative in their treatment of their low expectation students. The students responded in kind and produced even lower levels of performance than might have been anticipated given initial levels. On the other hand, unbiased teachers treated all their students similarly, which resulted in marked improvements in the performance of their low expectation students such that in the final measure of their performance, low expectation students were achieving at very similar levels to their high expectation peers.

You may remember that earlier in this book, I pointed out that generally expectation effects on student performance have been found to be small to moderate. However, this conclusion is based on studies where all teachers are considered together and then effects on their students are examined. As the findings with biased and unbiased teachers show (remembering that these constitute a little less than half of all teachers), biased teachers had marked negative effects on their students whereas unbiased teachers had positive effects on theirs. If the effects of biased teachers were to be combined with those of unbiased teachers and overall effects examined, it is likely that there would be small effects overall. However, as has been shown, there can be sizeable self-fulfilling prophecy effects in some classrooms but probably not in the majority. It is the classrooms in which there are large biasing effects with which we should be concerned. It is biased teachers who likely influence the findings in relation to expectation effects on students from particular groups (as described in the previous chapter). Worryingly, if the results were examined for only biased teachers among those overall samples, the effects on already disadvantaged groups may be much larger than generally recorded in the literature.

HIGH AND LOW DIFFERENTIATING TEACHERS

Another researcher who has developed a systematic program of research based around teacher beliefs that moderate expectancy effects is Rhona Weinstein. For many years, Weinstein has concentrated her efforts on identifying and researching teachers she calls high and low differentiating.[5] Her high differentiating teachers align most closely with the biased and over-reactive teachers described above whereas her low differentiating teachers are more like unbiased and proactive teachers. High differentiating teachers are those who treat high and low expectation students very differently, whereas low differentiating teachers make little discrimination in their interactions with students.

As reported in Chapter Two, Weinstein was interested in the final stage of the expectation model presented in the first chapter – whether and how students knew that their teacher had high or low expectations for them.[6,7] She found that, overall, students reported that high achievers were favored by teachers whereas low achievers were not.[5–10] Students reported that teachers revealed high expectations for high achievers and more autonomy in the choice of, and completion of, learning experiences. In contrast, low achievers were often criticized and were closely monitored by teachers. The different ways in which students were treated fell into six major areas: Grouping, materials and activities, evaluation, motivation, student responsibility, and class relationships. Ways in which high and low expectation students were treated in these key areas were outlined from the student perspective in Chapter Two. In this chapter, teacher reports of their differentiation and their reasons for treating students differently or similarly will be the focus.

Differentiation did not occur in all classrooms. In the classrooms of high differentiating teachers, high and low expectation students were treated very differently. In the classes of low differentiating teachers, all students were treated similarly. Importantly, of 30 classrooms in which measurements took place, the descriptions below pertain to the two classrooms measured highest and lowest in terms of student reports of differential treatment.[11] So again, these more extreme classrooms are a minority but are classes in which teachers are likely to have large positive or large negative expectation effects.

Observations in the classrooms of high and low differentiating teachers, and interviews with them, confirmed that their beliefs and practices differed markedly in the six key areas listed above which students had originally identified. The differences in their practices and beliefs will be described below with the practices and beliefs of high differentiating teachers presented first.

Grouping of students. High differentiating teachers assigned students to ability groups, and the teachers believed that high and low expectation students needed very different learning activities. Students were seated in their ability groups and there was little interaction between those in the different groups. High differentiating teachers made ability salient in the classroom by frequently referring to high versus low achievers or high versus low ability groups. At times they clearly expressed frustration towards the low achievers, not only criticizing them but also publicly deriding and humiliating them. In contrast, in the classes of low differentiating teachers, students were seated and worked in mixed ability groupings where students were expected to help and support each other. The teacher did not make ability salient in the classroom and treated all students equally.

The curriculum. Because of the teachers' beliefs related to ability grouping, high differentiating teachers designed very different activities for those who were considered high and low ability. High expectation students were often given individual projects to work on and, at times, the students chose what they wanted to work on. They were given a lot more autonomy and independence than other students. In contrast, the students defined as low ability were frequently given skills-based worksheets to complete. The activities were often repetitive. High differentiating teachers kept a close watch on the low achieving students and monitored their work. When work was not completed on time, these students were likely to be punished. Low differentiating teachers had all students completing very similar activities and students were often expected to collaborate on tasks. Students who were perceived as disinterested or unmotivated might be paired with enthusiastic students to work together. All students were asked high-level questions and a high quality curriculum was provided to all students.

Student evaluation. High and low differentiating teachers also held contrasting beliefs in relation to the ways in which they believed that students should be evaluated. High differentiating teachers believed that ability was fixed, that is that students were born with a certain amount of intelligence and little could be done to alter that. In other words, there was only so much a teacher could do to help students because if they did not have sufficient intelligence they would not be able to learn the material anyway. Hence, these teachers placed limits on students' capabilities. High differentiating teachers focused on the weaknesses of students. Beliefs such as these also exonerated high differentiating teachers from taking responsibility for student learning; if students made only limited progress, this was a function of their intelligence, rather than anything to do with the classroom instruction. Low differentiating teachers viewed learning quite differently. They believed that intelligence was malleable and that often low achievers simply needed encouragement and support in order to improve their academic performance. This belief led to low differentiating teachers taking responsibility for student learning. When students did not grasp a concept in the way that the teacher had hoped, blame was not assigned to the student. Instead, the low differentiating teachers found new ways to teach the concept. They focused on students' strengths and used those to build on.

Motivating students. High and low differentiating teachers also motivated students differently. High differentiating teachers mostly used extrinsic rewards. Students were awarded points, certificates, and other rewards when they achieved at high levels. These rewards reinforced the status of students in relation to their perceived abilities; high expectation students were well-regarded and rewarded, low expectation students were not. In this way, students were encouraged to outdo their peers. Low differentiating teachers, on the other hand, focused on students mastering skills. By providing a wide variety of interesting tasks for all students, the low differentiating teacher also encouraged intrinsic motivation. Although low differentiating teachers also used points to reward students, these were achieved by the mixed ability groups working together collaboratively and supporting each other, rather than for individual success.

Student responsibility. High differentiating teachers viewed their role as one of academic director. These teachers took charge of the learning in the classroom. High differentiating teachers provided students with assistance when needed and corrected their work if necessary. Peer interaction and support was minimal. The teacher maintained high levels of control over all students. Low differentiating teachers appeared to view their primary role quite differently. They believed that the teacher's role was primarily as a facilitator and socializer. Students could use each other as resources. Further, they had considerable responsibility for their learning, for evaluating their own work in terms of quality as well as that of their peers, for helping others in the classroom, and for completing a range of tasks collaboratively. All this, contributed to a class climate that reflected a community of relationships.

Classroom relationships. Perhaps not surprisingly by now, the class climate of high differentiating teachers was very negative. It was one of competition and constant threats about being moved to a lower group. Students were not admonished for name-calling or laughing at others, and mostly, low achieving students were often publicly humiliated by the teachers. Parents were mentioned as threats if students misbehaved or did not complete tasks. The climate of low differentiating teachers was far more collegial. All students were treated with dignity and respect. Students were trusted to complete tasks and low differentiating teachers often used humor appropriately with students to encourage them to complete tasks or to remain engaged. Parents were involved as helpers in the class and low differentiating teachers also used them as resources, for example, in teaching about different cultures. Similarly, low differentiating teachers enabled their students to interact with and work alongside other classes. By fostering collaboration and collegiality within the classroom coupled with developing broader relationships with parents and other classes, low differentiating teachers fostered a sense of community and support within their classrooms.

At this point, it should probably be said that Weinstein took the principles and practices of low differentiating teachers and used them, in partnership with teachers, principals, a school district and a charter organization to develop a high expectation high school for first-in-family to go to college.[12] The high school, now in its 12th year, has shown inspiring results for its students, demonstrating that the setting of high expectations and the implementation of the principles of low differentiating teachers can work equally well in a high school as in an elementary school. High expectations, the elimination of ability grouping (or tracking), coupled with high levels of support from committed and passionate teachers have shown that minority students from impoverished backgrounds can all realize their dreams and graduate with offers to a four-year college.

HIGH AND LOW EXPECTATION TEACHERS

Although much of the research has focused on differential expectations for individual students (and teacher differences in their propensity to produce such expectancy effects), little attention has been paid to classroom level expectations, and how teachers differ in whether they hold high or low expectations for all their students. My own observations of teachers, interviews with them, and measurement of their beliefs have shown this to be an omission within the literature. Hence, my research has targeted this largely understudied phenomenon of class level expectations and its effects on student outcomes. Whereas Brophy and Good, Babad, Weinstein, and I have all studied teacher differences, my own work has uniquely focused on class-level expectation effects (and teacher differences therein).

My own interest has always been with, what I term, high versus low expectation teachers. My focus is, therefore, on the teachers themselves. What do I mean by that? Almost all of the research has concentrated on the idea that teachers have high expectations for some students and low expectations for others. I am not denying that this occurs. However, when I began my research journey, I was interested in the idea that there were some teachers who had high expectations for all their students whereas others would have low. As I indicated earlier, I had been an elementary school teacher for a number of years. For much of that time I had worked in low socioeconomic areas. When I was the deputy principal, I went into a lot of classrooms. I also had access to student records. I was convinced that I had seen these high expectation teachers; wonderful examples of caring professionals who worked tirelessly with their students, had a real passion for teaching, and, most importantly, had high expectations for every single student. In the classes of these teachers, students scored much higher on standardized tests by the end of the school year than did students in other classes of the same age group.

Therefore, when I began reading the teacher expectation literature, I was looking for research that had focused on high and low expectation teachers, rather than students. There was virtually none, with perhaps one early exception.[1] The idea had certainly been mooted, and there was a claim that high expectations for whole classes may have larger effects on student outcomes than the effects on individuals within a class.[13] However, no one had systematically researched the possibility that such teachers might exist. But whether high or low expectation teachers had been researched or not, I was convinced I knew some!

I was able to identify high and low expectation teachers. My initial studies began with six high expectation teachers and three lows from a pool of 24 volunteers. Interestingly, the proportions of around one-quarter of teachers being identified as high expectation and one-eighth being low have been similar across many studies that I have since conducted. You might remember that the biased and unbiased teachers of Babad and the high and low differentiating teachers of Weinstein were also a minority. So, as with Babad and Weinstein, I am researching a small percentage of teachers at either end of the spectrum of teaching capability – those making large positive differences for students and others where students make few gains after being in their classes. There is, of course, the greatest proportion of teachers in the middle, many of whom are also highly effective teachers. They just do not fit my categorization. Their students make good progress each year, but not exceptional progress, as in the classes of high expectation teachers. However, their students also do not make the very limited gains of those with low expectation teachers.

I originally defined high expectation teachers as those who had high expectations for all their students, and the students made large gains over the academic year. Low expectation teachers had low expectations for all their students and, in one of the classes in my initial studies, the students made negative gains compared to where the students were in relation to national averages at the beginning of the year. In the other two classes, the gains were very small across one year. Further, in the classes of high expectation teachers, students became a little more confident in their capabilities over the academic year in both reading and mathematics whereas in the classes of low expectation teachers, the students' self-beliefs in both reading and mathematics dropped substantially. This meant that although there were no differences in the self-beliefs of students with high or low expectation teachers at the beginning of the year, there were substantial differences by the end of the year.

I interviewed high and low expectation teachers and also observed them several times working with their students. There were quite stark contrasts in their beliefs about teaching and what supports student learning, and these were evident in their practices. The differences in their beliefs and practices are epitomized in the descriptions below which represent a summary of the overarching differences between high and low expectation teachers. Meet Harriet, a high expectation teacher, and Laura, a low. I have grouped their beliefs and practices under three major headings: Grouping and learning experiences, goal-setting, and class climate. Please note that some of the quotations found in this section of the book can also be found in Rubie-Davies, C. M. (2015).[14]

GROUPING AND LEARNING EXPERIENCES

The ways in which high and low expectation teachers both grouped their students and taught them differed in a variety of ways. I am going to focus on: Flexible grouping, learning experiences, open-ended questions, and extended explanations.

Flexible grouping. Harriet did not ability group her students for learning activities for core subjects like reading and mathematics. This was a surprise because we have a very long tradition of within-class ability grouping in New Zealand, especially in reading. It is how things have always been done! Students are sorted into ability groups very early in the school year and sometimes before school has even begun, based on student achievement for the previous year. Harriet had made a conscious decision not to ability group her students for their learning experiences, despite pressure from her principal. She explained: "The children can choose the activities that they do, so they are not grouped for actual activities." In her class, all children were exposed to high level learning opportunities:

> I think everybody has to be exposed to it [more advanced activity] or else I am differentiating and I think the effect will be difficult on the children who may not be quite ready for it, but you know, they are still listening and they are still absorbing.

Laura, however, had very different views about ability grouping and the need to maintain those groupings for learning experiences: "They [low achieving students] wouldn't be able to cope with a task that I had set for the high ability so I do that to cater for where they are at."

Learning experiences. Because students were not ability grouped in Harriet's class for their learning activities, the student experience would have been very different in her class, compared to that for students in Laura's class. In Harriet's class, learning experiences were arranged in a variety of ways. Sometimes students worked together on activities in self-selected groups or they might be paired with high and low achieving students working together. At other times students completed whole class or whole group activities (based on seating groups). Students often chose their own activities and all the activities were levelled within them, for example, there might be a range of books around a common theme but students could select whatever they wished to read. Harriet explained another way in which she organized her students:

> Like if we are making a booklet, they are all making a book. Some of them are making it for themselves. Some of them are making it to teach others with and things like that. I try to get them all to do roughly the same sort of activity but try not to make it obvious that they're doing [different things] – well trying to differ the parts within that activity for each group rather than them all doing totally different work.

In this way, all students had the opportunity to be challenged and extended, and ability was not made salient in the classroom every day. In some New Zealand classrooms, teachers put reading levels on the classroom wall with student names beside the levels, so it is very obvious to students every single day where they fall in the hierarchy. One argument for ability grouping is that the high ability students will miss out or not be extended (although there is no evidence that this is the case) and Harriet also seemed to be aware of this when she said:

> For the high ability . . . to develop independence in their learning, the children can go to the learning center and do the problem solution chart and really think about what they have read and things like that. The chart is there for everyone but mostly only the children working at higher levels will use it.

But she was also aware of the need to provide challenging activities for her low achieving students: "They need activities that are challenging so they are motivated. If I don't make them independent as well [as the high achieving students], they won't learn to run by themselves. They'll always need the teacher."

Harriet also seemed to be of the view that students' intelligence was not fixed, that is, all students could improve and that rates of development for all students could vary at times:

> I think some children often they come in, they take time to get going and then they just shoot off and they could make that accelerated learning and yeah I think other children might just be at that plateau and then take off. I mean I just think anything is possible.

Laura had quite different views about the tasks she provided for her high achievers:

> I would be looking at more independent-type activities for my high-ability children compared to the low ability children. Yes, I think just for my high-ability group I would be looking at more complex tasks, tasks that they would have to work on in a more independent way.

In contrast, when referring to the types of tasks that the low achieving students completed, she said: "A lot of repetition, every day . . . "

Ability grouping, in and of itself, and the differentiating of learning opportunities portrays a fixed view of intelligence. Students are placed in a particular ability group because they have a certain amount of intelligence whereas others are placed in a different group because their intelligence is different. Laura's comments about the types of activities her students completed reflect that fixed view and are very different from Harriet's who was providing opportunities for all her students to make large gains.

Open-ended questions and teacher response. Harriet asked lots of open questions of her students, and she asked them of all students, for example, when introducing a reading book: "What do you think a noodle head might be?" and students went on to explain their response. Often when Harriet asked a question, if a student was having difficulty responding, she would encourage and prompt them in some way to help them think further.

Laura did not ask many high level questions of her students. When she did, she was selective about who she chose. Most of her questions were those requiring a factual answer so students were either right or wrong: "What's the formula for finding area, Celine?" and "Show me the line of symmetry in this design, Michael." Importantly, when students did not know the answer, Laura rarely supported students to a response. Instead, students were effectively dismissed. She frequently told students that they were wrong and then either gave them the answer herself or immediately asked another student. Hence, students in her class were not prompted to think more deeply but, perhaps more importantly, may have become wary of answering questions when they knew that they could be embarrassed if the response was not correct. They were learning that an incorrect answer was not acceptable; in Harriet's class an incorrect answer was an opportunity to promote learning.

Extended explanations. As teachers, we are often told that we talk too much – and that is probably true! Teachers are generally fairly social beings. However, interestingly, Harriet spent far more time introducing concepts and ensuring that students had a good understanding of new ideas before sending them off to complete tasks. One day she was introducing a reading book: "This story is called *Homespun*. With that title what do you think it is going to be about?" She then showed the students the various pictures in the book before they began any reading. She had also been to her local craft shop and brought a spinning wheel and wool into the classroom. Each student in the group she was working with had a turn on the spinning wheel. These students were city kids; Harriet knew that they most likely would not be familiar with the whole of process of shearing sheep through to knitting a jersey. However, her students had a very good understanding of what that book was going to be about before they set about reading it! She also linked to prior learning: "Who can tell me about the Milky Way, from the other day?" In this way, she ensured that children remembered their previous learning before moving onto something new.

Laura did not put in this type of effort into introducing new material. One day, one of her lower groups were being given a new book; she said: "This book is called *Budgerigars*. Take a book and your worksheet and go and read it and then answer the questions." Even at the time, I thought that at least some of these students were unlikely to be familiar with budgerigars and would likely struggle with what they were being asked to do. Similarly, there was not the scaffolding of student learning nor the linking to prior knowledge evident in the examples above in Harriet's class.

It seemed fairly clear that the more exciting learning experiences in Harriet's class, coupled with the ways that she supported learning were likely to be more beneficial than Laura's approach whereby even when students were dealing with what may have been unfamiliar topics, they were not scaffolded or supported in their learning.

GOAL SETTING

Several components of the teaching fell under what I am terming goal setting because, ultimately, they were related. This section largely includes practices and beliefs that were specific to Harriet. This is simply because they were not evident in Laura's class at all. Where possible I have described what Laura did in contrast to Harriet's reasons for her practice.

As I have already described, Harriet often gave her students choices related to their learning experiences. This meant that all students were challenged and there were lots of exciting activities available for students. This was motivating for students. However, clearly this gives students a certain level of responsibility for their learning. Harriet managed this by setting very clear goals with her students. Every Friday, she would pull aside students, talk about their learning and what they believed they had achieved and then together they would set new goals for the student's learning. She did this with around one-quarter of students each week so that students were setting new goals monthly. Thus, Harriet monitored the students' learning closely and both in these goal setting sessions, as well as frequently during lessons, students were given very clear feedback based on their learning in relation to their goals. Further, the focus on individual goal setting meant that students were concentrating on mastering skills; the motivational structure was intrinsic rather than extrinsic. Hence, the overall categorization of goal setting was also related to building student autonomy and motivation, as well as teacher feedback and monitoring.

Goal setting. As described above, Harriet regularly set goals with her students. She spoke about her use of goal setting:

> Well, I think they have to know what they can do. We talk about goal setting, and resetting goals and going forward again and then coming back and reflecting on it . . . Actually knowing what it is that they are learning to do is really powerful and potent. So it's easy for children to know what they are working on and I try to always be specific about why we are doing it because I just think they need to know when they have made personal progress.

Laura had set goals with her students at the beginning of the year. However, there was no regular re-visiting and re-setting of goals and the goals seemed more focused on behavior than learning. Occasionally, Laura would ask her students to "put your hand up if you have achieved your goals." But even when students thought they had achieved their goals they were not advised or helped to reset them, nor was there any teacher checking that the goals had, indeed, been achieved.

Student autonomy. One of the ways in which Harriet developed student autonomy was through giving students choices in their learning experiences. As described above, this enabled all students to challenge themselves. As with goal setting, student choice also meant that students had considerable responsibility for their learning. Harriet was aware of this: "I might give them a range and say, we could work on this, or we could work on that, what would you like to work on? So that they have got to take ownership of it." She saw her role much more as a facilitator of student learning, there to support and guide but also there to teach students to become independent.

Laura, however, was more of a director of student learning. She made all the decisions for her students. She decided what her students would learn (and this differed depending on student groups), who they would learn it with, and how they would complete the activities.

Motivation. Harriet used a variety of methods to motivate her students. When students disliked a particular subject or were struggling, she worked with student interests to try to motivate them:

> I have a couple of really low kids who aren't interested in math and just don't like it, but they love cricket [a game played with a ball and bat] so we found some batting averages activities and they just loved it and they worked on that problem for 40 minutes until they worked it out . . . Sometimes it's finding activities that they are interested in, rather than just doing something they are not into.

Harriet was also aware of the detrimental effects on student self-belief when students were assigned to particular ability groups. Her focus was very clearly on developing students' skills:

> I just think that having mixed ability ... is really important so that they have all got a contribution to make and their skills, their particular skills are valued this way because if you have a pecking order in the class, motivation can go out the window and you won't see star charts and stuff like that in my room. I am more interested in intrinsic motivation than extrinsic so I don't have them.

Laura used a different approach. Although she did not openly comment on student levels, students were well aware of who was in the top group and who was in the bottom. She often praised students who scored highly on tests so in her class, gaining teacher acknowledgement was largely through performance.

Teacher feedback. In Harriet's class, feedback was focused on developing student skills: "Lovely way he said 'screamed.' It sounded like screaming without yelling it out" and "Well done; it was quite a long story but you listened really well and worked out what a noodle head might be." It was common in Harriet's class for students to be receiving feedback not only during their specific goal setting sessions but also on a daily basis as she monitored their learning.

Laura did praise and criticize her students at times. This tended to be her way of providing feedback to her students. However, this was often quite vague, for example, "Well done" or "Good boy," and therefore was not informative for students in terms of their learning.

Teacher monitoring. Although Harriet gave her students a lot of independence in terms of the learning activities, as outlined above, she did monitor her students closely. This monitoring was occurring not just once a month but daily:

> The lessons are needs-based in that I give a lot of feedback to children and in the talking you know about them, and the

> watching, the observing, that's the time when I actually identify their learning or lack of learning and what skill they need to sharpen next, so then I weave that into whatever I am doing.

Laura did not keep as close an eye on her students. She did do some in-class tests at times. These were used to see whether her groups were ready to move onto the next level in reading or how well they had mastered a mathematics unit. But that information was not used for future planning in the way that Harriet used her understandings of student learning. Instead, Laura used the information to decide if her groups were ready to move to the next level in reading or mathematics, and almost always whole groups moved together from one level to another. It was rare for students to change groups because assessment was at the group rather than individual level. In this way the gaps between her highest and lowest achievers were likely sustained or possibly exacerbated, whereas in Harriet's class, students moved individually as they were ready, and often students moved very rapidly from one level to another because they were making regular gains.

CLASS CLIMATE

Harriet built a very warm classroom climate. She was supportive and caring towards her students and was always respectful of them. She also built student relationships by seating her students in mixed ability groups that changed often. Students worked collaboratively on a regular basis and were expected to support each other. Because the groups were changing frequently, this meant that all students worked with each other over time which helped to develop a sense of classroom community. As Harriet explained: "They seem very supportive of each other . . . I think consciously they try and help each other if they know they need help and things like that." It may have been that the students were also happy to assist others because the focus was on developing

Teacher Differences

individual skills rather than on trying to do better than other peers. Harriet was careful about how she distributed her praise:

> There are times when we applaud, you're a good artist and you are good at throwing the ball, and I am very, very careful that they all have an opportunity to shine in something ... I think for self-esteem it's important to be high ability in something.

Harriet was also seemingly very spontaneous in her praise of the whole class with many examples of statements like: "You are fabulous" and "Gosh you guys are amazing." In that way, her praise related to all the students in the class and individuals were not singled out. As well, statements like this serve to make everyone in the class feel good and, in turn, students were then even more likely to want to please Harriet.

In Laura's class some of the learning interactions with the teacher were negative rather than positive. Examples are: "No, you don't do it like that. You should know that by now." Clearly, statements such as this are not likely to improve the recipient's self-esteem which was something Harriet was conscious of. Laura also openly criticized or embarrassed her students at times, for example: "Okay, this is William; [teacher demonstrates] don't do that, always look forward." A further example of individual criticism was: "Look, he hasn't got his ears in the right place" [said when one child was not listening to an instruction]. An example of class criticism was: "You're not in the zoo, so you don't have to sound like a herd of animals." There were no statements like this in Harriet's class.

The ways in which teachers managed their students also differed. Harriet was much more likely to to use techniques that pre-empted the types of behavior that she wanted: "Let's see which groups can move quietly to their desks and begin working quickly," and another example, "What lovely quiet girls over there and these boys here as well." Her behavior management was very positive and this further contributed to the warm atmosphere that was very evident in Harriet's classroom. Even when there was some misbehavior, Harriet focused on the students who were doing the right thing: "Ah, that red table, you're remembering your quiet voices [said when students at another table were being noisy]." Of note, as well, almost all of Harriet's management focused on groups or the whole class; she did not often single out individuals.

On the other hand, Laura used preventive statements infrequently. She was far more likely to react to student misbehavior and often what she said was focused on individuals who were singled out for admonishment: "You know the rules, no talking;" "Sit down" (which was shouted at one student); "Don't be last;" and "No, you're not listening to the instructions."

The different decisions that Harriet and Laura made about how they set up learning in the classroom and their beliefs about how to organize students and behavior management, influenced the general class climate, the relationships of the teacher with her students, and the relationships of the students with each other.

MOVING FORWARD

Overall, the use of flexible grouping by high expectation teachers, the effective instructional practices used, the variety of learning activities and the leveling within them, the clear goal setting with students premised on student choice and motivation, and on teacher feedback and monitoring, and the warm class climate, probably all contributed to the rapid learning gains that were being made by the students and possibly also to their positive self-beliefs. These practices formed the basis of the Teacher Expectation Project (TEP: http://www.education.auckland.ac.nz/en/about/schools-departments/ldpp/ldpp-research/ldpp-research-projects/teacher-expectation.html).[14] I wanted to find out whether or not it was possible to have all teachers adopt the practices of high expectation teachers in the key areas of grouping and learning experiences, goal setting and class climate, and measure the effects on student outcomes.

The TEP was a large scale experimental study in which 84 teachers were randomly assigned to either the intervention or the control group. Over a series of four full-day professional development workshops, the intervention group were taught the practices of high expectation teachers. These were then instituted into their classrooms and the research team visited schools regularly in order to help support teachers but also to enable teachers to share their successes with each other. The control group, on the other hand, did not receive any form of intervention until the second year of the study. This enabled us to measure any differences that the intervention had on student achievement and beliefs.

The workshops also consisted of teachers being taught about nonverbal behavior and how expectations can be portrayed to students. Videoing of teachers before they came to the workshop enabled them to view their behaviors. This videoing of teacher interactions and behaviors while they were teaching was highly successful and led to teachers being videoed three further times during the three-year project. Teachers were sent their videos following each recording so that they could continue to self-analyze their progress. Videoing of teacher practice is something that is very easy to do nowadays and something that I strongly recommend. It is because videoing of practice seemed to have such marked effects on teacher practice that I have recommended it at various places in this book. Teachers can video themselves on their phones or tablets, and if the video is for their own purposes then there is no reason to put on a show for whoever they believe might see the video. It is for them alone. Teachers always find it amazing to discover some of the patterns of nonverbal behavior that they display, and although it is not easy to change nonverbal behavior, recognition is the first step. Teachers can focus on particular nonverbal behaviors, set goals for themselves to improve, they can systematically examine their teaching and their interactions with students, there are a wealth of possiblities.

TEP teachers worked together to plan how to introduce the practices of high expectation teachers into their classrooms. They brainstormed the types of activities that they could set up in reading and mathematics that would avoid ability grouping but would ensure that all students were learning and had appropriate choices of learning activities. One example that is relatively easy to introduce is a theme box whereby several books are gathered together around a common theme (e.g., space, dinosaurs, wild animals, sports heroes – the list is endless). The books within the box are leveled so some are easier, some are more challenging. The point is that students choose those they wish to read. There are not certain books for particular students. Another box could have poem cards or even poetry books, and again, students select those they wish to read. Even traditional readers can be used with a box having multiple levels and students can pair up to read to each other. If teachers enjoy reading to their students, then a novel can form the basis of a project for students to investigate. For example, a story set during wartime might form the basis for a project on the role of animals in previous wars or what happened to children who were evacuated during the second World War. There are an enormous number of teacher websites that offer a multitude of exciting, fun activities for students and most of these can be adapted so that students work in mixed ability groups and so that flexible grouping is a feature of the classes. That is, sometimes students might work on a class project, other times they could work in small groups on something of common interest, other times they might be in pairs, other times the focus might be a particular skill with particular students, other times they might work with their seating groups. There are many ways of grouping students and an endless number of activities that can create a vibrant, exciting learning environment for students.

Teachers also learned how to use various types of goal setting with their students, for example, SMART goals. We are fortunate in New Zealand that we have a standardized test, e-asTTle (https://e-asttle.tki.org.nz/About-e-asTTle/Basics) which also provides information in curriculum objectives about what each student already knows and what they need to learn next in reading, mathematics and writing, so teachers immediately have goals that can be used with students as the next steps in their learning. As suggested earlier, one way in which teachers can monitor student learning is to set aside one day each week (approximately one-quarter of students each week) when students work individually with the teacher to set new learning goals. While some students are working with the teacher, for example, in reading, the rest of the students can be allowed to choose reading activities. Provided that the routines are well established and students are practiced at choosing their own learning experiences, they will understand that they need to work quietly.

For the final area, class climate, teachers brainstormed ways to increase positive feelings into their classes. Improving student collaboration and a sense of community plays a large part. Teachers and students can work together at the beginning of an academic year to set the premises on which they want their classroom to function. For example (and taken from one intervention teacher's class[14]), "We will treat other people the way we want to be treated," "We will use kind words to each other," "We will be persevering and determined and never give up," and "We will be helpful towards each other." When students have input into a class agreement about the values that will be promoted in their classes, they are much more likely to adhere to them. Of course, it is important that the teacher also agrees to act in the ways decided upon. Another activity that worked well was a brag wall whereby students could write about something they were especially proud of and illustrate it if they wished or add a photo. They did this on bricks (pieces of light card that the teacher had painted and cut to an appropriate size), put them on the wall and then added to it over time. This was so successful that even the teacher aides joined in! In another class, students created booklets illustrating times when they felt especially happy or proud or grateful or peaceful or loved and then stored these in their own personal space (a desk or locker) so that on a bad day, they could be reminded of better times and the possibility of better days to come. Another suggestion from intervention teachers was just to have fun with students occasionally, whether it be a sing-along, letting students dance to music, having a joke sesssion, and so on. Again, the possibilities are endless.

In the first year, the TEP resulted in large learning gains for the students in the classes of intervention teachers compared with the gains of the students in the control group, equivalent to 28 percent additional learning in mathematics over one year. Importantly, there were no differences between intervention and control groups at the beginning of the year.[14,15] We also examined whether some groups had benefitted more than others. For example, it was possible that students in one particular ethnic group had made enormous gains, sufficient to show large gains across the whole intervention group but actually only really pertaining to one group. This was not what was found. Instead, no matter what school students were from or what grade (Grades 3–8), no matter what socioeconomic group, ethnic group, or gender, all students benefitted.[16] Further, we were able to show that the more that teachers implemented the practices of high expectation teachers, the greater were the gains for their students.[15] Because of the success of the project, in the second year of the project, control group teachers were also taught the practices of high expectation teachers so that their students could also benefit.

In addition intervention teachers evaluated the project and provided feedback.[17] They commented on different aspects of the project. For example, one teacher in talking about allowing students to choose their activities, said: "I am getting more confident in allowing students to choose the activities they want to do, choose who they work with, letting go of control." Another teacher reported that giving students choices had "given them greater ownership of the activities and raised the bar in their learning." Teachers also reported benefits of flexible grouping: "I grouped less confident readers with more confident readers and I found that both groups really enjoyed this. The struggling readers had buddies to support them and the more capable readers thrived with the responsibility."

Although goal setting constituted the final workshop, most teachers had also endeavored to implement it and were finding that it had helped student learning:

> I used goal setting and reflections on achievement each Friday and found it beneficial in improving the students' autonomy over their own learning. They became much more articulate and reflective about what they needed to improve or work on.

Teachers were also enthusiastic about the changes that they had made to their class clmate:

> I believe that working on my class climate has had a significant impact on . . . the reading levels in my class. After changing/implementing strategies from the workshop, I could see huge changes in the students' self-management and their feelings towards learning and BELIEVING in themselves.

Teachers noticed other changes in their students:

> I have been certain to affirm each student by way of feedback, their successes and next steps. The dedication and interest shown in their work has meant positive attitudes towards their learning which has, in turn, helped with the classroom climate.

They found that having students change desks on a regular basis was also having effects:

> ... every two weeks the children move desks and it means they have all got to know one another and there is more harmony in the classroom.

After all the work on teacher expectations based on correlational work (Are teacher expectations related to student characteristics? Is there an association between teacher interactions with students and their expectations of students?), the TEP provided experimental evidence that teacher expectations and their actions can be enhanced in important ways to improve student achievement. Overall, the TEP showed that when randomly selected teachers implemented the practices of high expectation teachers into their classrooms, their students benefited both in terms of learning as well as leading to a more harmonious class environment. Teachers also reported enjoying teaching and their classes more. The factors that constituted the intervention (flexible grouping, goal setting, and class climate) work together to create a high expectation classroom where both teachers and students like to be. The removal of ability groups means that ability is not salient every day, students do not become disheartened, and all students are encouraged to work at and beyond their level, to challenge themselves and to learn. Boring, repetitive activities for low achievers disappear. Students have clear learning goals designed to help them master skills. Worrying about someone else's achievement is not a focus of these classrooms. The teacher has excellent relationships with students and shows that she cares about every single one of them. Students work together to support each other. They know every other child in the class. The class is a happy place in which to work as evidenced by motivated, engaged students who have excellent relationships with both their teacher and each other.

As predicted in earlier work,[13] it seems that expectations at the class level may have greater effects on student learning than expectations for individuals. However, whether at the class or at the individual level, teachers need to consider the power of their expectations to transform students and their learning. Expectations are transmitted to students every day. Students are astute observers and assimilate those messages. It is important that as far as is possible, every child in every class is made to feel valued and worthwhile. Students need to be supported and encouraged to be the best that they can. High expectations for every child coupled with high expectation teaching practices can accelerate learning progress for all students, improve their motivation and engagement, and broaden their life chances and future opportunities.

REFERENCES

1. Brophy JE, Good TL. *Teacher-student relationships: Causes and consequences.* New York: Holt, Rinehart & Winston; 1974.
2. Babad E. Preferential affect: The crux of the teacher expectancy issue. In: Brophy J, ed. *Advances in research on teaching: Expectations in the classroom.* Vol 7. Greenwich: JAI Press; 1998:183–214.
3. Babad E, Bernieri F, Rosenthal R. Nonverbal communication and leakage in the behavior of biased and unbiased teachers. *Journal of Personality and Social Psychology.* 1989;56:89–94.
4. Babad E, Inbar J, Rosenthal R. Pygmalion, Galatea and the Golem: Investigations of biased and unbiased teachers. *Journal of Educational Psychology.* 1982;74:459–474.

5. Weinstein RS, Marshall HH, Brattesani KA, Middlestadt SE. Student perceptions of differential teacher treatment in open and traditional classrooms. *Journal of Educational Psychology.* 1982;74:678–692.
6. Weinstein RS, Marshall HH, Sharp L, Botkin M. Pygmalion and the student: Age and classroom differences in children's awareness of teacher expectations. *Child Development.* 1987;58:1079–1093.
7. Weinstein RS, Middlestadt SE. Student perceptions of teacher interactions with male high and low achievers. *Journal of Educational Psychology.* 1979;71:421–431.
8. Brattesani KA, Weinstein RS, Marshall HH. Student perceptions of differential teacher treatment as moderators of teacher expectation effects. *Journal of Educational Psychology.* 1984;76:236–247.
9. Kuklinski MR, Weinstein RS. Classroom and grade level differences in the stability of teacher expectations and perceived differential treatment. *Learning Environments Research.* 2000;3:1–34.
10. Kuklinski MR, Weinstein RS. Classroom and developmental differences in a path model of teacher expectancy effects. *Child Development.* 2001;72:1554–1578.
11. Weinstein RS. *Reaching higher: The power of expectations in schooling.* Cambridge: Harvard University Press; 2002.
12. Weinstein RS, Worrell FC, eds. *Achieving college dreams: How a university-charter district partnership created an early college high school.* New York: Oxford University Press; 2016.
13. Brophy JE. Research on the self-fulfilling prophecy and teacher expectations. *Journal of Educational Psychology.* 1983;75:631–661.
14. Rubie-Davies CM. *Becoming a high expectation teacher: Raising the bar.* London: Routledge; 2015.
15. Rubie-Davies CM, Peterson ER, Sibley CG, Rosenthal R. A teacher expectation intervention: Modelling the practices of high expectation teachers. *Contemporary Educational Psychology.* 2015;40:72–85.
16. Rubie-Davies CM, Rosenthal R. Intervening in teachers' expectations: A random effects meta-analytic approach to examining the effectiveness of an intervention. *Learning and Individual Differences.* 2016;50:83–92.
17. McDonald L, Flint A, Rubie-Davies CM, Peterson ER, Watson P, Garrett L. Using an intervention to change teacher expectations and associated beliefs and practices. *Professional Development in Education.* 2014,42:290–307.

Five
What Has Been Learned and Where To Next?

This book has provided a history of the teacher expectation construct, discussed aspects of the process of teacher expectations, and highlighted the importance of considering teacher factors when thinking about teacher expectations. Teachers are critical to student success. They vary enormously in their effects on students but when high expectation principles are applied into any classroom, all students can benefit in substantial and meaningful ways.

The self-fulfilling prophecy, first proposed by Merton[1] in 1948, has been investigated in laboratory, business, armed forces, medical, courtroom, police line-up, witness, and educational sites. Through investigations in these hugely varying settings, the construct of the self-fulfilling prophecy has consistently been shown to exist and to affect the outcomes of those who are the targets of particular expectations. It is a concept broadly accepted within social psychological circles. When Rosenthal[2] applied the concept to education, his study brought with it both proponents and critics. However, the careful and detailed observational recording of teacher behaviors by Brophy, Good and others[3–8] that followed the initial study, clearly showed how teachers differentiated in their interactions with students for whom they had high or low expectations. Babad[9,10] was able to show that this differentiation existed not just in the types of learning support that was provided to students but also in the ways that teachers emotionally favored some students over others. Further, the work of Weinstein,[11–16] in particular, clearly showed that students recognized that some teachers treated students very differently depending on the teachers' expectations for the students. Researchers also became interested in the precursors of teacher expectations; that is, what student characteristics might influence teacher expectations. A number of student characteristics were found to induce teachers' expectations, including, but not limited to, ethnicity, social class, gender, and special needs status.

Importantly, although much of the data within teacher expectation research was aggregated across all teachers, it was always acknowledged that there would be variation among teachers. That is, some teachers were likely to have much larger expectation effects on students than others. Further, my own research[17–20] has shown that whereas many previous and current studies have focused on the negative consequences of low expectations, there are teachers with high expectations for all their students who have meaningful positive effects on student outcomes – both academic and psychological. Importantly, the Teacher Expectation Project (TEP) showed that all teachers could be trained in the practices of high expectation teachers and raise the achievement of all students.[21–23]

The teacher expectation field is one that has always been embedded in social justice concerns. The study of teacher expectations is about the promotion of fairness and equitable educational opportunities for all students. Many studies in the field have pointed out ways in which teacher expectations can have negative consequences for students and therefore lead to outcomes that are unfair and inequitable. The field has contributed much to understandings of how low teacher expectations can undermine the life chances of students and of how some teacher practices probably inadvertently contribute to exacerbating these negative effects. Much has been learnt about teacher behaviors and student characteristics that can exacerbate differences between students, and how low teacher expectations can contribute to a widening of the gap between high and low expectation students. It is now time to focus on what we have learned from the literature about how high expectations and the implementation of high expectation principles can lead to a narrowing of the gap between high and low achievers.

The recent book of Rhona Weinstein and Frank Worrell[24] provides compelling evidence of how a university partnered with a charter school district to create a high expectation school, Cal-Prep. The school is based around high expectation principles. CalPrep was, and still is, a school for first-in-family to go to university. It does not cherry pick only the best students; the majority of the students are from disadvantaged minority groups, and yet, all graduate with an offer to a four-year college. The book shows that when teachers believe in their students, institute appropriate support, and have high expectations for every single student in their classes, all can succeed in an educational system that had previously condemned such students to drop out and failure. Notably, many of the students come into CalPrep at Grade 9 level at least four years behind in achievement in the core curriculum areas. In just a few short years, they not only make up the ground that they have lost, but, in many instances, they surpass it. Several CalPrep students now attend leading universities in the United States; the school, based on external standardized testing, is one of the top performers in California – and that is compared to all schools, not just those in disadvantaged areas.

Equally as important, and in elementary and middle schools, rather than a high school, the TEP showed that when randomly selected teachers were taught the practices of high expectation teachers, all students benefited. Student achievement in mathematics improved 28 percent, in one year, above what was achieved by students whose teachers were not taught the high expectation practices. Further, the evidence showed that the more that teachers engaged in the high expectation practices, the greater were the gains for their students. Importantly, this was an experimental study so we are able to claim that the intervention (the high expectation practices that teachers were taught) caused the improvements in student achievement. It will be important that this study is replicated in other settings so that the findings can become generalized to other countries. Nevertheless, the very similar findings of Weinstein and myself about what constitute high expectation principles is already promising. In settings across the world from each other, the United States and New Zealand, there is now strong evidence that high expectation principles make a profound difference to student learning when implemented into classrooms.

In moving forward, it is important that the messages about what constitute high expectation principles and how these can be instituted into classrooms are passed on within teacher education programs. It is disturbing that it was recently reported that very few teacher education programs include any systematic training in high expectation principles.[25] When these principles clearly have positive effects on student learning, they should become core ideas taught to all pre-service teachers.

It is also essential that schools move beyond the idea of ability grouping in any form whether within or between classes. This categorizing and labeling of students immediately makes achievement salient; students soon come to understand that some students are more valued than others, depending on the groups they are assigned to. Differential teaching interactions result from ability grouping, with negative consequences for many, and students are given different learning opportunities, depending on their group. Often, as we have seen in this book, it is already disadvantaged students who are even more disadvantaged by the education system and the practices that it promotes. Grouping of students is a large contributor to the academic trajectories of students, and, in many countries, can seriously impede students' opportunities for entering a host of occupations. I find it ironic that, at a time when some teachers proclaim that they have a growth mindset (a belief that all students can improve their intelligence), they still use ability grouping (which is very much based on the idea of innate ability, a fixed mindset).

The TEP[21-23,26] taught teachers how to teach core subjects without within-class ability grouping (a practice that is entrenched in New Zealand elementary and middle schools). An important component of the high expectation principles incorporated into the teaching at CalPrep is that all classes are mixed ability; there is no tracking. Both the CalPrep and TEP programs have been successful in significantly raising student achievement, and, importantly, as the TEP showed, *all* students benefited. This means it was not just low achievers or disadvantaged students or minority groups who became more successful; *all* students benefited.

Tracking or within-class ability grouping is not the only teacher expectation principle that is important to consider in making our education systems more equitable and more effective, but it is a core consideration. In moving forwards, ability grouping is a practice that needs to be eliminated from our schools. Just because it is what has always been done does not mean that it is best practice.

Other core high expectation principles, such as a focus on building relationships in the classroom, teacher-student and student-student, are far more genuinely instituted as a regular part of classroom life when all students in the class are valued, and there are high expectations for everyone. In an environment where students understand that they are expected to collaborate and support each other, where their seating groups change regularly, and where they work with and support all their peers, a classroom community is created. There is a safe environment of trust. Students understand that mistakes are learning opportunities.

They learn that they are there to support each other. Similarly, goal setting, monitored regularly by teachers and focused on individual mastery of skills, helps to lessen the salience of ability in classes. Students become highly motivated as they strive to meet their own goals without the burden of comparison, and in an environment where all are challenged and supported.

Finally, the idea of teachers regularly monitoring their own verbal and nonverbal interactions with students by videoing lessons is a powerful way of keeping check on the equity and fairness of teacher treatment of students. If this is something that becomes part of school culture where teachers can share clips that they choose in a collegial environment of support, teachers can work together to create class environments in which all students can succeed. A further interesting finding in the TEP was that the more that school management were involved and invested in the project, the greater were the gains for the students whose teachers were in the project. This shows that it is not just students who need a collaborative environment if they are to be successful; teachers also need to feel supported and safe.

This book has told the story of teacher expectations, and of how and why the research developed as it did. It has presented the important findings and directions in the field. However, it has also shown the important contribution that individual teachers can make in opening up future possibilities for students. When teachers have high expectations for all students and institute high expectation principles, there is every possibility that all students can make academic and social gains that may not previously have been conceived of as achievable. It is important to believe in every student, to develop the talents of each and every one of them, and to create a future in education where every child has every opportunity to succeed at the very highest levels.

USEFUL WEBSITES

www.random.org
http://arb.nzcer.org.nz/ (Assessment Resource Banks)
www.tki.org.nz/ (Go to 'Learning areas' and click one of the categories for ideas)
http://assessment.tki.org.nz/Assessment-tools-resources/The-New-Zealand-Curriculum-Exemplars
http://www.readingrockets.org/article/82
https://accountability.madison.k12.wi.us/teacher-team-toolkit
https://www.youtube.com/watch?v=9JPCrP6GdEI
https://www.youtube.com/watch?v=Ib9DUTL34Pc&t=189s

REFERENCES

1. Merton RK. The self-fulfilling prophecy. *The Antioch Review.* 1948;8:193–210.
2. Rosenthal R, Jacobson L. *Pygmalion in the classroom: Teacher expectation and pupils' intellectual development.* New York: Holt, Rinehart & Winston; 1968.
3. Brophy JE, Good TL. Teacher-child dyadic interaction system. *Mirrors for behaviour: An anthology of observation instruments continued* Vol A. Philadelphia: Research for Better Schools, Inc; 1970.
4. Brophy JE, Good TL. Teachers' communication of differential expectations for children's classroom performance: Some behavioral data. *Journal of Educational Psychology.* 1970;61:365–374.
5. Brophy JE, Good TL. *Teacher-student relationships: Causes and consequences.* New York: Holt, Rinehart & Winston; 1974.
6. Cooper HM, Good TL. *Pygmalion grows up: Studies in the expectation communication process.* New York: Longman; 1983.
7. Good T. Which pupils do teachers call on? *Elementary School Journal.* 1970;70:190–198.
8. Good TL, Brophy JE. Changing teacher and student behavior: An empirical investigation. *Journal of Educational Psychology.* 1974;66:390–405.
9. Babad E. Preferential affect: The crux of the teacher expectancy issue. In: Brophy J, ed. *Advances in research on teaching: Expectations in the classroom.* Vol 7. Greenwich: JAI Press; 1998:183–214.

10. Babad E. *The social psychology of the classroom*. New York: Routledge; 2009.
11. Weinstein RS. Student perceptions of schooling. *The Elementary School Journal*. 1983;83:286–312.
12. Weinstein RS. Perceptions of classroom processes and student motivation: Children's views of self-fulfilling prophecies. In: Ames R, Ames C, eds. *Research on Motivation in Education*. Vol 3. New York: Academic Press; 1989:187–221.
13. Weinstein RS. Children's knowledge of differential treatment in school: Implications for motivation. In: Tomlinson TM, ed. *Motivating students to learn: Overcoming barriers to high achievement*. Berkeley: McCutchan; 1993:197–224.
14. Weinstein RS. *Reaching higher: The power of expectations in schooling*. Cambridge: Harvard University Press; 2002.
15. Weinstein RS, Marshall HH, Brattesani KA, Middlestadt SE. Student perceptions of differential teacher treatment in open and traditional classrooms. *Journal of Educational Psychology*. 1982;74:678–692.
16. Weinstein RS, McKown C. Expectancy effects in "context:" Listening to the voices of students and teachers. In: Brophy J, ed. *Advances in research on teaching. expectations in the classroom*. Vol 7. Greenwich, Connecticut: JAI Press; 1998:215–242.
17. Rubie-Davies CM. Teacher expectations and student self-perceptions: Exploring relationships. *Psychology in the Schools*. 2006;43:537–552.
18. Rubie-Davies CM. Classroom interactions: Exploring the practices of high and low expectation teachers. *British Journal of Educational Psychology*. 2007;77:289–306.
19. Rubie-Davies CM. Teacher beliefs and expectations: Relationships with student learning. In: Rubie-Davies CM, Rawlinson C, eds. *Challenging thinking about teaching and learning*. Haupaugge: Nova; 2008:25–39.
20. Rubie-Davies CM. Teacher expectations and perceptions of student attributes: Is there a relationship? *British Journal of Educational Psychology*. 2010;80:121–135.
21. Rubie-Davies CM. *Becoming a high expectation teacher: Raising the bar*. London: Routledge; 2015.
22. Rubie-Davies CM, Peterson ER, Sibley CG, Rosenthal R. A teacher expectation intervention: Modelling the practices of high expectation teachers. *Contemporary Educational Psychology*. 2015;40:72–85.
23. Rubie-Davies CM, Rosenthal R. Intervening in teachers' expectations: A random effects meta-analytic approach to examining the effectiveness of an intervention. *Learning and Individual Differences*. 2016;50:83–92.

24. Weinstein RS, Worrell FC, eds. *Achieving college dreams: How a university-charter district partnership created an early college high school*. New York: Oxford University Press; 2016.
25. Babad E. The final word. In: Rubie-Davies CM, Stephens JM, Watson P, eds. *Routledge international handbook of social psychology of the classroom*. London: Routledge; 2015:385–394.
26. McDonald L, Flint A, Rubie-Davies CM, Peterson ER, Watson P, Garrett L. Using an intervention to change teacher expectations and associated beliefs and practices. *Professional Development in Education*. 2014;42:290–307.

Glossary

Academic trajectory	The learning gains of students over time. The trajectory may be steep, steady or fairly flat indicating the degree of progress.
Acculturation	A process whereby minority and immigrant groups learn to understand and adopt the majority culture of the country where they live.
Bias	Strongly held views about particular groups of people that are not adjusted for individuals or in line with available evidence.
Biased teachers	Those who are easily swayed in their views of students based on demographic or stereotypical information.
Carryover expectation effects	The teacher expectation effects of the Grade 2 teacher, for example, that affect student achievement several years later, that is, the effects continue for several years.
Class climate	The psychological, emotional, and social elements of the classroom that combine to form a particular atmosphere in every classroom.
Compounded expectation effects	The expectation effect of a particular teacher, perhaps the Grade 2 teacher, added to the effect of the Grade 3 teacher, added to the effect of the Grade 4 teacher, and so on; the combined expectation effects of several teachers over several years on a student.

Critical incident	A comment from a teacher that has a marked effect on student self-beliefs for many years after the original incident. The effect can be positive or negative.
Differential interactions	Interacting in different ways with some students rather than others.
Dyadic communication	An interaction between two people; in education, a teacher and a student or student-student.
Emotional support	The ways in which teachers relate to, comfort and care for students as individuals.
Experimental studies	Studies that involve random assignment of one group of teachers who receive some form of intervention and a control group who do not receive any (or receive a different) intervention. In this way, variables such as student or teacher differences can be controlled and any differences can be credited to the experimental manipulation.
Explicit expectations	The expectations that teachers record on paper or computer for each individual student. Teachers have time to think about each student, before recording their views.
Externalizing behaviors	Behaviors that are negative and outwardly obvious, for example, aggression, hyperactivity, or disruption.
High differentiating teachers	Those who treat high and low expectation students very differently.
High expectation students	Those for whom teachers have high expectations relative to achievement.
High expectation teachers	Those who have high expectations for all their students relative to achievement.
Implicit expectations	The subconscious beliefs of teachers about student capability measured with an implicit bias test. Teacher response is instantaneous

Glossary

	and perhaps more reflective of actual beliefs than explicit beliefs.
Instructional environment	The ways in which teaching and learning occur in the classroom, the teaching methods used and the ways teaching and learning are structured.
Internalizing behaviors	Behaviors that may not be obvious such as anxiety, stress, withdrawal, or reticence.
IQ Test	A test designed to measure people's innate intelligence. Popular in the 1950s and 1960s, they went out of favor when it was discovered that many of the tests that had been used in schools were culturally biased.
Learning support	The ways in which teachers endeavor to promote student learning.
Low differentiating teachers	Those who treat high and low expectation students similarly.
Low expectation students	Those for whom teachers have low expectations relative to achievement.
Low expectation teachers	Those who have low expectations for all their students relative to achievement.
Naturalistic studies	Studies that take place in classrooms during regular day-to-day interactions between teachers and students.
Nonverbal behavior	The gestures, facial expressions, body language and voice tone of a person.
Overestimation	Teacher beliefs that particular students are achieving above where standardized test results show they are actually achieving.
Portfolio information	Documented academic and social progress details that are recorded and passed from one teacher to another each year.
Psychosocial environment	The psychological, emotional, and social elements of the classroom, often referred to as the class climate.

Pygmalion study	The first ever experimental study of teacher expectations.
Self-fulfilling prophecy effect	The effect on the target person of someone's initially false beliefs. For example, if a teacher expects a child to make limited learning gains over one year, the teacher may give the child lower level learning opportunities than s/he is capable of completing. Over time, the child's learning opportunities are constrained and s/he would probably learn less than if s/he had been given more challenging learning opportunities.
Self-fulfilling prophecy	An originally false belief that leads the person with the false belief to interact with the target of their beliefs in particular ways.
Skinner box	A box that can have an embedded maze. In laboratories, animals are put into the Skinner box and they learn to tap a lever in order to receive food. When the box has a maze, the lever would be located at the end of the maze.
Stereotypes	Generalized beliefs about particular groups of people.
Teacher expectations	The beliefs that teachers hold about the progress teachers think their students will make over time (often one year).
Underestimation	Teacher beliefs that particular students are achieving below where standardized test results show they are actually achieving.
Wait time	The length of time that a teacher waits for a student to answer a question before intervening in some way.

Index

Note: 'N' after a page number indicates a note; 'f' indicates a figure; 't' indicates a table.

ability grouping: arguments for 125; and fixed vs. developmental mindset 125–6; vs. flexible grouping 123–4, 140; and high vs. low differentiating teachers 117; and high vs. low expectation teachers 130–1; negative effects of 146–7; and social class 74–8; student perceptions of 46, 58
academic trajectory: critical incidents' effect on 50; defined 152; and self-fulfilling prophecy effect 78; and social class 74–8
acculturation 152
accuracy of teacher expectations 14–16
ADHD 92–4
African American students. See minority students
assessment: and goal setting 137; and high vs. low differentiating teachers 118; and high vs. low expectation teachers 131–2; student perceptions of 47. See also feedback
attention 35
attractiveness 98–9
Australia 69–70

autism 92–4
autonomy 48, 119, 128–9, 130

Babad, E 43, 49, 112–13, 143
bias: and attractiveness 98–9; defined 152; and English language learners 96–8; and ethnicity 62–72, 94–5, 98; and gender 78–83; negative vs. positive 25; and personality 99–100; shaped by portfolio information 62; and social class 72–8; and special needs students 83–94; and student names 98; study of, in teachers 112–15
body language. See nonverbal behavior
boys: behavior of 81–2; literacy of 81; in mathematics 78–9; in science 79–80; and teacher expectations 32, 52. See also gender
Brophy, JE 10–14, 12f, 31–40, 110–12, 143

CalPrep school 145, 147
Canada 65
carryover expectation effects 23–4, 152

Index

class climate: defined 13, 152; effects of, on students 43–4; of high expectation teachers 89; and high vs. low differentiating teachers 119–20; and high vs. low expectation teachers 132–4; implicit messages of, to students 13–14; importance of 147–8; and Teacher Expectation Project (TEP) 137–8, 139. *See also* psychosocial environment

classroom relationships 48–9, 119–20, 132–3

compounded expectation effects 22–3, 25–7, 152

critical incidents: and academic trajectory 50; defined 153; effects of, on students 27–8, 50–1

criticism of students 34–5, 50–1, 133

curriculum 117–18

deafness 89–90

differential interactions: defined 153; for high vs. low expectation students 40; student perceptions of 43, 49, 58. *See also* bias; teachers, high differentiating

disabled students. *See* special needs students

Draw-a-Person test 113

dyadic communication 31–2, 153. *See also* feedback

dyslexia 90–1

emotional/behavioral difficulties (EBD) 91–2

emotional support: defined 153; for dyslexic students 91; impact of, on student outcomes 40; for low vs. high expectation students 41–5, 49; for sexually abused students 96

English language learners, and teacher expectations 96–8

ethnicity 62–72. *See also* minority students

experimental studies 153

explicit expectations 13–14, 71, 90–1, 153

externalizing behaviors 91–2, 153

eye contact 38

family circumstances 95–6

feedback: and high vs. low expectation teachers 131; for low vs. high expectation students 35; and student perceptions 47; and Teacher Expectation Project (TEP) 140. *See also* assessment

fixed mindset 147

flexible grouping 123–4, 136–7, 139

foster care 96

friendliness: for low vs. high expectation students 38. *See also* emotional support

gender: and behavior of boys vs. girls 81–2; and literacy 81; and mathematics 78–9; and science 79–80; and teacher expectations 78–82

giftedness 94–5, 98

girls: behavior of 81–2; literacy of 81; in mathematics 78–9; in science 79–80; teacher expectations of 32. *See also* gender

goal setting 128–32, 137, 139

Good, TL 10–14, 12f, 31–40, 110–12, 143

grades and assignments 37–8

grouping. *See* ability grouping; flexible grouping

growth mindset 147

Index

'halo effect' 114

implicit expectations 13–14, 71, 72, 90, 153. *See also* bias
incarceration 96
instruction, grouping for. *See* ability grouping
instructional environment 12f; as conveying messages to students 13–14; defined 13, 154; student perceptions of 53–7
instructional methods 39
intelligence, as fixed vs. developing 125–6, 147
interactions, individualized 37
internalizing behaviors 154
IQ test: defined 154; Draw-a-Person test 113; and *Pygmalion* study 8–9
Israel 65–6

Jacobson, Lenore 8

learning disabilities 86–9
learning experiences 46–7, 124–6
learning support: and Babad's study 143; defined 154; for high vs. low expectation students 40–1; student perceptions of differential 43
literacy 81
long-term effects of teacher expectations: and carryover effects 24–5; and compounded effects 25–7; and Dutch study 24–5; and inaccuracy of expectations 15–16; Rist study on 19–23

mathematics 78–9, 97
Merton, RK 143; and self-fulfilling prophecy effect 4
minority students: in Australia 69–70; in Canada 65; effects of teacher expectations on 5; and giftedness 94–5; and inaccuracy of teacher expectations 15; in Israel 65–6; in New Zealand 70–1; and *Pygmalion* study 9; and Rist study 19–23; and self-fulfilling prophecy effect 4; and student names 98; and teacher expectations 62–72; in United Kingdom 66–8; in United States 64–5; in Western Europe 68–9
Moscardini, L 86–9
motivation 47–8, 118–19, 130–1

names, of students 98
naturalistic studies 84, 154
New Zealand 70–1
nonverbal behavior: of biased teachers 114; defined 154; of high differentiating teachers 36, 38, 52; study on 43; and Teacher Expectation Project (TEP) 135–6; value of monitoring 148

Oak Elementary School 8
open-ended questions 126–7
overestimation 23, 154
over-reactivity 111, 113

personality 99–100
portfolio information 62, 154
practice and revision 39
praise 35, 51, 133
proactivity 111
psychosocial environment 43–4, 154. *See also* class climate
Pygmalion study: criticisms of 8–9; defined 155; and minority students 9; origins of 4; replication attempts 16–17; Rosenthal and Jacobson's methodology 8; support for 9

question response 33–4

reactivity 111–12
reinforcement, inappropriate 34
Rio, NT 51–7
Rist, Ray 19–23
Rosenthal, Robert 6–7, 8, 112, 143

science 79–80
seating, classroom 36
self-belief 99–100, 130–1
self-fulfilling prophecy 5–6, 22, 155
self-fulfilling prophecy effect: and academic trajectory 78; of biased teachers 115; and Brophy and Good study 110; in classroom setting 143; defined 155; Merton's study on 4
sexual abuse 95–6
Skinner box 7, 155
social class 72–8, 98
social justice 144–5
social skills 99–100
Sorhagen, NS 77
special needs students: ADHD and autism 92–4; dyslexic 90–1; emotional/behavioral difficulties (EBD) 91–2; hearing impaired 89–90; learning disabled 86–9; studies of, and teacher expectations 88–9; and teacher expectations 83–94
stability, of teacher expectations 17–19
stereotypes: of deaf students 89; defined 155; of ethnicity in Australia 69; and expectations 6; of gender 79, 80; and over-reactive teachers 111; and reactive teachers 111–12; teacher resistance to 101, 110. *See also* bias

students: attractiveness of 98–9; and classroom relationships 48–9; critical incidents' effects on 27–8, 50–1; English language learners 96–8; ethnicity of 62–72; explicit vs. implicit messages to 13–14; family circumstances 95–6; gender of 78–82; giftedness 94–5; initiation by 38; motivation of 47–8, 118–19, 130–1; names of 98; perceptions of teacher expectations 24, 43, 45–58, 116; personality 99–100; self-belief of 99–100, 130–1; social class of 72–8; special needs 83–94. *See also* boys; girls; minority students; special needs students
students, high expectation: defined 153; perceptions of teacher expectations 43, 45–58; Rio's study on 51–7; teacher expectations of 31–40; teachers' emotional support of 41–5, 49. *See also* students
students, low expectation: defined 154; perceptions of teacher expectations 43, 45–58; Rio's study on 51–7; teacher expectations of 31–40; teachers' emotional support of 41–5, 49. *See also* students
student selection 35–6

teacher demands 36–7
Teacher Expectation Project (TEP) 134–9, 144, 145–7
teacher expectations: accuracy of 14–16; of boys vs. girls 32, 52; Brophy and Good study on 31–40; defined 1, 155; effects of, on minority students 5; long-term

effects of 16, 19–28; model for effects of 10–14, 12f; Rio's study on 51–7; stability of 17–19; student perceptions of 43, 45–58, 116; studies of 2–3

teachers: biased and unbiased 112–15; over-reactive 111, 113; proactive 111; reactive 111–12; videotaping of, as intervention 135–6

teachers, biased 152. *See also* teachers, high differentiating; teachers, low expectation

teachers, high differentiating: and ability grouping 117; and assessment 118; attention of 35; Brophy and Good study on 31–40; and class climate 119–20; and classroom seating 36; and criticism of students 34–5; and curriculum 117–18; defined 153; demands of, for low vs. high expectation students 36–7; eye contact 38; and feedback 35; friendliness of 38; and grades and assignments 37–8; and inappropriate reinforcement 34; and individualized interaction 37; and instructional methods 39; nonverbal behavior of 36, 38, 52; and practice and revision 39; and praise for students 35; and question response 33–4; selection of students 35–6; and student initiation 38; and student motivation 118–19; student perceptions of 43, 45–58; and wait time 33; Weinstein's study on 115–20. *See also* teacher expectations; teachers, biased

teachers, high expectation: and assessment 131–2; and class climate 89, 132–4; defined 153; and extended explanations 127–8; and feedback 131; and goal setting 128–32; and grouping 123–4, 130–1; and learning experiences 124–6; and open-ended questions 126–7; praise by 133; studies of 122–41; and Teacher Expectation Project (TEP) 134–9, 145–7

teachers, low differentiating: and ability grouping 117; and assessment 118; and class climate 119–20; and curriculum 118; defined 154; and student motivation 118–19; Weinstein's study on 115–20

teachers, low expectation: and assessment 131–2; and class climate 132–4; criticism by 133; defined 154; and extended explanations 127–8; and feedback 131; and grouping 123–4, 130–1; and learning experiences 124–6; and open-ended questions 126–7; studies of 122–41

Teacher Treatment Inventory 51

TEP. *See* Teacher Expectation Project (TEP)

theme box 136

tracking. *See* ability grouping; academic trajectory

underestimation 23, 155
United Kingdom 66–8
United States 64–5

videotaping 135–6

wait time 33, 155
Weinstein, RS 143–4, 145; on critical incidents 27; study by, on student perceptions 45–9; study by, on teacher expectations 51–2; study on high and low differentiating teachers 115–20
Western Europe 68–9
Worrell, FC 145

# Taylor & Francis eBooks

Helping you to choose the right eBooks for your Library

Add Routledge titles to your library's digital collection today. Taylor and Francis ebooks contains over 50,000 titles in the Humanities, Social Sciences, Behavioural Sciences, Built Environment and Law.

Choose from a range of subject packages or create your own!

Benefits for you

- » Free MARC records
- » COUNTER-compliant usage statistics
- » Flexible purchase and pricing options
- » All titles DRM-free.

Benefits for your user

- » Off-site, anytime access via Athens or referring URL
- » Print or copy pages or chapters
- » Full content search
- » Bookmark, highlight and annotate text
- » Access to thousands of pages of quality research at the click of a button.

 **Free Trials Available**
We offer free trials to qualifying academic, corporate and government customers.

eCollections – Choose from over 30 subject eCollections, including:

Archaeology	Language Learning
Architecture	Law
Asian Studies	Literature
Business & Management	Media & Communication
Classical Studies	Middle East Studies
Construction	Music
Creative & Media Arts	Philosophy
Criminology & Criminal Justice	Planning
Economics	Politics
Education	Psychology & Mental Health
Energy	Religion
Engineering	Security
English Language & Linguistics	Social Work
Environment & Sustainability	Sociology
Geography	Sport
Health Studies	Theatre & Performance
History	Tourism, Hospitality & Events

For more information, pricing enquiries or to order a free trial, please contact your local sales team:
www.tandfebooks.com/page/sales

 | The home of Routledge books | **www.tandfebooks.com**

For Product Safety Concerns and Information please contact our EU representative GPSR@taylorandfrancis.com
Taylor & Francis Verlag GmbH, Kaufingerstraße 24, 80331 München, Germany

www.ingramcontent.com/pod-product-compliance
Lightning Source LLC
Chambersburg PA
CBHW050123020526
44112CB00035B/2360